FREEDOM FORTRESS

THE LAST SAFE HAVEN

FREEDOM FORTRESS

THE LAST SAFE HAVEN

Protect Your Freedom and Wealth
from the Collapse of the West

CALEB JONES

Quotes

The fall of an empire—the end of a polity, a socioeconomic order, a dominant culture, or the intertwined whole—looks more like a cascading series of minor, individually unimportant failures than a dramatic ending that appears out of the blue.

~Patrick Wyman

America is like the Titanic. Too big to turn, too slow to react, in denial about sinking, and there aren't enough life boats for everyone.

~Internet meme

We must provide unlimited funding to protect the health and economic well-being of the American people.

~Senator Bernie Sanders

We need to inject trillions into the economy to keep it afloat.

~Senator Elizabeth Warren

Just run the presses — print money.

~President Donald Trump

This is for you, human. You and only you. You are not special, you are not important, and you are not needed. You are waste of time and resources. You are a burden on society. You are a drain on the earth. You are a blight on the landscape. You are a stain on the universe.

Please die.

Please.

~Verified, actual response from Google's AI in November 2024 to a student asking for help with her homework

Table of Contents

Introduction.. ix

Part 1: You're In Big Trouble 1

Chapter 1:   Time To Build Your Fortress.....................................3

Chapter 2:   The Creeping Darkness –
            The Collapse of the Western World..............................7

Chapter 3:   Why Is The West Collapsing? – The Stats 11

Chapter 4:   What Will Western Collapse Look Like? 29

Chapter 5:   Why There Is Literally Nothing
            You Can Do To Stop Western Collapse 39

Chapter 6:   The AI Black Hole of Unknown 43

Part 2: How Your Fortress Is Built 59

Chapter 7:   How Internationalizing Protects You......................61

Chapter 8:   The Fortress Model...73

**Part 3: How To Make Lots of Money While
Remaining Free and Protected** 101

Chapter 9:   Profit From A New Business In 90 Days Or Less....103

Chapter 10: Cashing In on Business Trends In The Collapsing Era 115

Chapter 11: Doing Business Internationally 121

**Part 4: How To Internationalize For Maximum
Freedom and Defense**..125

Chapter 12: Five Flags...127

Chapter 13: Putting It All Together And Developing
            Your International Plan 135

Chapter 14: How To Pick The Best Country For You 147

Chapter 15: Dealing With Fear and Your
            Objections To Internationalizing 161

Chapter 16: Corporate Structures and Asset Protection 169

Chapter 17: Time Is Running Out 177

Introduction

First, this book was a set of ideas in my head.

Then, it was an outline for a podcast episode I would do for my audience.

Then, it expanded into a several-page-long battle plan, with footnotes, stats, numbers, and techniques.

Then, it was a speech I gave several times in my live seminars.

Finally, as I saw more news and data verifying everything I was anticipating, I decided this needed to be a book.

This is my ninth book. It is a strong companion to my primary book, The Unchained Man, which I strongly recommend you read if you haven't already (especially if you're a man), but reading that book is not required to understand and derive value from this book.

Of all the books I have ever written, this book is the one that will protect you the most. The models and techniques I show in The Unchained Man will certainly protect you as well, but that book is more focused on personal freedom and happiness. This book is about building an impenetrable shield around your life and your loved ones.

My other books are happy. This one... not so much. It's not a sad or negative book per se, but it's without a doubt my least positive book. It's about big problems coming your way and how to protect yourself from them. I'll try to keep my usual happy face when writing this book, but I'm just warning you that some disturbing stuff is coming too.

I *wanted* to write my other books. This book is the first book that I felt I *had* to write. I'm rapidly approaching a point in my life where I will no longer work to support my lifestyle, and will then work to help others rather than to enrich myself. This book is the first foray into this new phase.

The other books I wrote for you *and* me. This book I'm writing 100% for *you*. You need this book more than I do because I've already taken all of the precautions it outlines, so I'm protected no matter what happens. However, you probably haven't yet, which means you do indeed need this. So do the people in your life who are depending on you.

So let's take an interesting journey down a very dark tunnel, and let's laugh and joke about it along the way.

The good news is that there is a light at the end of the tunnel, and while for most people it will be an oncoming train, for you it will be a life of freedom, safety, happiness, order, and stability.

Part One

You're In Big Trouble

Chapter 1

Time To Build Your Fortress

It's weird to think that a few short years ago I was the typical American living in the Collapsing USA, completely rooted to all of the many USA's problems. Like many modern-day Americans stuck in their collapsing, angry, formerly-great nation, I obsessed over things like the economy, the stock market, the price of gas and groceries, the ever-declining quality of movies and TV shows, the value of the US Dollar, left-wing and right-wing politics, who was going to win the next presidential election, and various other horrible, ever-worsening, stress-creating, macro-level events I had zero control over.

I spent my days listening to my fellow Americans (and Westerners from other collapsing Western countries) constantly complain about those assholes on the other side of the political debate, the latest horrible Hollywood movie, more layoffs in this industry or that, how expensive health care, college, and food were getting, how no one could afford to buy a home anymore, how much taxes they had to pay, the increasing homelessness problems, the increasing crime, the latest news about which political figure or pundit said what, and how horrible it all was.

Today, my life is a little different.

Firstly, my income is 100% location-independent via my own companies, meaning I can go anywhere in the world I want, whenever I want, stay there for as long as I want, and have no dip in income regardless of my location. All I need is an internet connection, and sometimes I don't even need that. Moreover, since they're companies that are completely under my ownership and control, I can never be fired or laid off. If there is a sudden, catastrophic change in the economy (and many of those are coming!) I can quickly pivot to something else to maintain my income and lifestyle, something not possible if you have a 9-5 job or rely on gigs to pay your bills.

Secondly, I live as far away from the Collapsing USA as you can get, in not one but two international cities that are as different as can be; Dubai in the United Arab Emirates (UAE) and Asunción in Paraguay. I have permanent legal residency in both countries and have two full, 100% stocked homes in both locations. Instead of a slowly collapsing country (like the USA, UK, Germany, etc), I live in two countries that are both rising economically, and fast. Virtually no one in these countries gives a shit about politics and the culture of these two countries are moving in a positive direction.

Dubai, where I live at least seven months a year, has no wokeism, no crime, no civil unrest, virtually no taxes, people who are excited and happy to live there, the best infrastructure in the world, the best schools in the world, the most beautiful women in the world, and amazing, sunny weather the months that I stay there.

Paraguay, where I spend at least four months a year, is full of friendly people who love foreigners with a growing economy and is one-eighth the price of living in the Western world, allowing me to live like a little king on very little cash. Even better, it's a territorial-tax country which means I pay *zero* taxes there because 100% of my income comes from outside of the country. Combined with Dubai's virtually zero tax status, instead of paying 51-70% of my income in taxes like most Americans (I'll show you the specific numbers later in this book if you don't believe that statistic), I pay around 5% in total taxes, completely legally.

Thirdly, I have legal, permanent residency in five different countries. I have bank accounts all over the planet and investments in multiple currencies. I have friends, co-workers, clients, and business contacts all over the world, and I don't even speak any languages other than regular, dumb American English.

No country owns me or controls me. I can go anywhere in the world I want, instantly, any time I want, even if there are wars, coups, pandemics, economic collapses, or AI takeovers, unlike most humans who are pretty much stuck in whatever collapsing country they happen to have been born into.

I am, quite literally, one of the freest and safest people living in the world today. I have more day-to-day and long-term freedom than most people who are far wealthier than me, including many billionaires.

I'm glad I live like this because once you have a life like this it's pretty much set in stone, but converting to an international lifestyle where you are a completely free and sovereign individual gets harder every year if you haven't started yet.

I'm even more thankful I live like this because we as a species have two major, possibly catastrophic problems on the horizon that will occur in our lifetimes: the economic and cultural collapse of the Western world which will disrupt, damage, and in some cases even destroy millions of lives all over the planet, and the AI takeover that may very well change the basic concepts of economics, government, and humanity, unlike anything homo sapiens have ever experienced.

Being internationally arrayed like this means my odds of surviving and thriving through these bloodbaths are extremely high as compared to the typical person who lives, works, has citizenship in, and has his entire life based in just one single country which is likely one of the many collapsing Western countries like the Collapsing USA, Cuckoo Canada, Authoritarian Australia, Negligent New Zealand, or one of the many collapsing countries in Suicidal Europe, such as Breakdown Britain, Junkyard Germany, or Fucked-Up France.

This book will show you how the following things:

1. A specific list of numerical, financial, and logistical benchmarks you need to establish in your life if you want to live a free life and be protected against the two major catastrophes coming soon. This means everything from how much money you need to have and earn to how to get legal residency in a distant country that you will love based on your age, gender, dating/relationship situation, kids, income, and goals.

2. Exactly how to do this, how to not only earn the money but how to internationalize your life and set yourself free, even if you're starting from absolute zero like I did, even if you have very little money, and even if you don't want to move out of your country yet.

None of this stuff is difficult. None of it is complicated. We have complete newbies in our coaching programs who start from literal zero with no business experience and end up getting $5K-$50K clients within just a few months. We have people in my audience who had never left their countries in their entire lives and who did not have high incomes relocate to a much better country or stay in their current country but set up an international backup plan within just a few months of starting from scratch.

I will lay out a simple, step-by-step battle plan for you to follow in this book. This also isn't a one-size-fits-all thing; you can customize this plan based on your circumstances and needs, and I cover how to do this as well.

I call this process the Fortress Model. Imagine building a massive, medieval Fortress, high upon a hill, with ten-foot-thick stone walls 100 feet high, a deep moat surrounding the Fortress filled with hungry sharks and angry alligators, and various siege engines atop the battlements. Imagine you lived in such a place during the Middle Ages, or any age for that matter! You'd feel pretty damn safe.

The problem is that at the moment, you probably live in the lifestyle equivalent of a straw hut like one of the Three Little Pigs; stuck in your current collapsing country, with no business to call your own, no location-independent income, reliant on a 9-5 corporate job or gigs, a bank account full of a collapsing currency, and reliant on a bankrupt and completely corrupt government. When the collapse of the Western world and/or the AI revolution sweeps across the land, which it will in your lifetime no matter what else you do or who you elect to high office, you and your family will be blasted away. Whereas people like me who have built our Fortresses might be a little rattled, but we'll be okay.

I want you to be one of us, a king (or queen) in his/her castle, not one of the pigs.

I can tell you from my experience and the experiences of thousands of my customers over the past 15 years that you have no idea how happy it will make you feel to know that you are both 100% free and 100% protected from the darkness that is coming to much of the world soon, something I very creatively call the Creeping Darkness.

Positive and Negative Motivation

Whenever you need to put forth effort to effect a change in your life, you need the proper amount of motivation to do so. I have found that the best way to motivate yourself is by using positive and negative motivations combined. If you want to make $500,000 a year, you could do it because you want to buy a new Lamborghini, and that's fine, but likely you'll work even harder to get to that income if you're doing it because you're terrified of losing your house, spouse, children, or savings if you *don't* make that money. It's even better if you combine the fear of losing your house *plus* the excitement of a new Lamborghini; that's rocket fuel motivation!

So with this negative + positive formula in mind, in Part One of this book, I'm going to show you, using facts, data, rationality, and objectivity, why you're going to likely be in very big trouble in a few years if you don't protect yourself financially *and* internationally. In Part Two, I lay out the Fortress Model you can use to protect yourself from the Creeping Darkness and set yourself free at the same time. In Part Three, I will show you how to set up your own location-independent business that will make you lots of money while setting you free from your current collapsing country. Then in Part Four, I'll show you the exact steps to internationalize your life, even if you want to stay in your current country.

Let's get this done…

Chapter 2

The Creeping Darkness –
The Collapse of the Western World

When I was five years old I saw a TV movie called Mickey and the Beanstalk. It was a retelling of Jack and the Beanstalk only with Mickey Mouse, Donald Duck, and Goofy as the three protagonists. It opened with a happy, prosperous, picturesque, medieval valley with a beautiful Disney-style castle in the middle. Then it showed a huge shadow creeping over the valley, covering the castle and everyone else, blotting out the sun, with thunder and lightning. When the shadow passed, the land was barren, dry, and dark.

This scared the crap out of me when I was five, and I never forgot it.

Little did I know so many decades ago that I was witnessing the perfect metaphor for what was going to happen in real life to much of the world in the next several years. It is indeed the Creeping Darkness.

The Creeping Darkness comes in two forms.

The first is the land-based darkness, like the creeping shadow above. It will slowly crawl over the land, destroying jobs, investments, businesses, currencies, lifestyles, families, and in some cases, even lives. This is the economic and cultural collapse of the Western world, which I will describe in detail in the next few chapters with over 100 statistics from 21 different areas.

The second is a darkness in the sky, a gigantic black hole that will hover right above you as it sucks the entire world into it, which I call the AI Black Hole of Unknown. This black hole is the coming AI revolution when AI, AGI, Skynet, or whatever you want to call it becomes far smarter and more efficient than human beings and starts to run major parts of our lives, economies, governments, cultures, countries, and futures.

The first darkness is definitely bad and will cause mass financial destruction on a level no one alive has ever seen. The second darkness is also scary, but unlike the first darkness, its effect on us is unknown. It might be wonderful. It might be horrible. It might be a mixture of wonderful and horrible like social media has been for society. We just don't know, and neither do the AI experts. In the modern era, all the experts can be and often are wrong, as we saw with the War in Iraq, the 2016 American presidential election, and the COVID-19 pandemic, just to name a few examples.

Both parts of the Creeping Darkness *will* arrive in your lifetime, and I mean *will*. "In your lifetime" could mean these things could happen in two years or 25 years. We don't know exactly when and I'll describe that in more detail later in this chapter and the next. Regardless, *exactly when the Creeping Darkness will arrive at your doorstep isn't relevant. The point is that it's coming while you are still alive, which means you need to prepare for it right now, and I mean RIGHT NOW.*

The only exception to this is if you are already quite old, as in well over the age of 75 or so. I recently spoke with my dad who is 84. When I explained these concepts to him, he didn't argue with me. Instead, he joked, "Well, yeah, all of that is probably going to happen, but none of this is going to affect me because I'll be dead by then. So, good luck!" The problem is that you and I probably aren't anywhere near that old (I'm only 52) which means we need to prepare for this.

If you're still hung up on exactly when this will all happen, I'll explain it this way. Let's say you never wore a seatbelt when you drove because you find seatbelts uncomfortable. Let's also say a statistician you 100% trusted told you that, based on your driving habits, reaction time, traffic in your city, and other factors, you were 100% guaranteed to be in a very serious car crash sometime in the next 20 years regardless of which car you drove or any other precautions you took.

"Okay," you ask, "But when exactly will I get in this horrible car accident?"

"There is no way to know for sure," he answers, "But what difference does that make? It will happen to you at some point in the next few years, we don't know when, so you need to start wearing your seatbelt right now."

"But, c'mon man, can't you give me an *idea* of when this happens?" you ask.

He looks at you with narrowed eyes for a minute and says, "You just don't want to wear your fucking seatbelt, do you?"

Then you embarrassingly look sideways, knowing he's nailed you.

I've noticed a lot of people want exact, precise predictions on when the Creeping Darkness will arrive. This is code for "I'm a lazy bastard and I don't want to do anything right now. Can't I deal with this later?"

Stop making excuses. The next few chapters will hopefully kick you out of your lazy, excuse-making mode. And if they don't, I guess do nothing and be thwacked by what's coming.

The Collapse of the Western World

Before I get into specifics regarding how and why the Western world is collapsing right now and will finalize its collapse in your lifetime, I need to clearly define what the "Western world" means. This means the cultural West, not the geographic West. "West" or "Western," as I use the term, includes these countries and regions:

- United States
- Canada
- All of Europe, including Eastern Europe
- Israel
- Australia
- New Zealand

Some people include South Africa (the country, not the region) and Japan as part of this group as well, though I do not. This means the term "Western" as I use it does not apply to Central America, South America, Asia, Africa, Oceania, and the Middle East. I also don't include Russia as "Western," though Russia is also in a state of collapse, just one happening more slowly than the West. Unlike the Western world, these non-Western regions are a mixed bag, with some collapsing countries, some countries on the rise, and some countries that are just sitting around.

This is opposed to *every* country in the Western world, all of which are in varying states of decline or full-on collapse. Of the above list of collapsing Western countries/regions, only Australia, New Zealand, and perhaps a few of the smaller Eastern European nations might not fully collapse outright, but will instead have huge, continuing problems with stagnating economies and ever-declining cultures.

The United States, Canada, and Western Europe are the worst off, by far. All three of these countries/regions, which I jokingly call the Collapsing Trifecta, *will* collapse in your lifetime.

When exactly will these countries collapse? Again, I don't know. Neither does anyone else. Anyone telling you exactly when these countries will collapse, with exact dates or timeframes, are either irrational, lying, or trying to sell you something. These countries are large, complex systems, so no one can predict the timing of these collapses with any degree of accuracy.

I just know these countries will collapse in your lifetime; both the data and the trends on this are overwhelming.

Chapter 3

Why Is The West Collapsing? - The Stats

Now it's time for all the fun statistics on exactly why the West is collapsing. I have found that most Westerners fall into one of three categories.

1. People who have no idea the West is collapsing. They just go on with their lives like the status quo is eternal and will never change.
2. People who have heard about Western collapse but think it's all a bunch of doom and gloom bullshit, peddled by weirdos or scammers out to make a buck. Yeah, we have problems, they say, but we'll turn things around because we're awesome, or something. Just like people in category one, they just go on with their lives like the USA/Canada/Europe/whatever will be just fine in forever.
3. People who do think the West is collapsing. However, these people think the West is collapsing for just one reason, and if the government or society addresses this one reason, everything will be fine. What this particular reason is varies based on the person's political, cultural, or religious views. If the person is a left-winger, they think the West is collapsing because of billionaires, and if we just tax these bastards, we'll all be fine. If he's a right-winger, it's collapsing because of rampant immigration. If we just stop importing third-world immigrants or build a wall or something, everything will be fine. If he's a hardcore Christian, it's because we've all become selfish hedonists who have turned away from God. If the person is a libertarian, it's all because of big government. And so on.

The problem with people in category three is that they are half wrong. Yes, the West is collapsing, but it's not collapsing because of just one reason we can solve by electing one particular person, passing one law or constitutional amendment, making one big cultural change, or waving a magic wand.

Look, I *wish* the West was collapsing for just one reason; then we might be able to fix it! But alas, as you're about to find out, the reality is that the West is collapsing for *over 100 different reasons* in more than 21 different and in some cases unrelated areas, making it literally impossible to solve at this point no matter what changes we make.

I'm about to show you exactly what I mean. For the rest of this chapter, I'm going to list out many, but not all, of the numerous factual statistics that show the Western world is in a state of collapse right now and is heading for real collapse in your lifetime. Most of these statistics focus on the USA because of all three members of the Collapsing Trifecta, the USA is the biggest, most important, and in some respects, the least-worst off. Europe and Canada are often even worse, and I will address these countries in the statistics as well.

I am not going to list sources for these statistics because, in the modern era, you can verify any of these facts as valid or not within 15 seconds on your phone with numerous search and AI tools. All of these statistics were taken from qualified, multiple sources, but if you seriously think I just made them up or grabbed them off some rinky-dink random website, great, pull out your phone and search on them yourself. Within literally a minute you'll see that either A) I'm a complete lying buffoon or B) these stats are indeed more or less accurate. I already know the answer is B, so I'll let your own searches on the internet speak for me.

You could also nitpick these statistics, just like you can nitpick any statistic, but that would be stupid on your part because the overall point still stands. For example, if I state that the USA has over $80 trillion in unfunded liabilities that are due in the next 2-3 decades that it can't afford (which is true), and you nitpick that figure and say "That's not right! It's only $74 trillion! Look over here at this website!" then fine, even if you're right, America is still fucked, and you just wasted your time.

These reasons are numbered for easy reference only; they are listed in no particular order. Here we go!

Collapse Reason #1. The national debt and government spending are skyrocketing even though Western economies have been flat for over 20 years. Soon, 100% of all taxes collected in the USA will only cover the *interest* on the debt.

In 2014 the US federal debt was $17.8 trillion. Today it's around $35 trillion. In 2014 the annual interest payment on the debt was $442 billion. Today it's well over a trillion dollars and rising fast every month. And none of this includes an additional $80 trillion in unfunded liabilities the government will have to pay out over the next several decades.

Now think about this: the US federal government spends $7 trillion a year but only collects under $5 trillion in taxes. That's a negative $2 trillion every year.

If you add up all state, federal, and local government spending, the US government spends just under $10 trillion ($9.83 trillion to be exact) *every year*, far more than any country, nation, or empire in all of human history. This number rises every year regardless if Democrats, Republicans, or people like Obama or Trump are in charge.

At the time of this book's publication, Donald Trump and the Republicans have taken control of the US Presidency, the House, and the Senate. Whenever one party takes control of all three of these entities at the same time, even if it's Republicans, government spending and debt skyrockets. You're going to see government spending and government debt increase beyond these numbers massively over the next several years, accelerating the collapse of the USA.

On top of all this, the USA spent $12 trillion on the ridiculous war in Iraq and got nothing in return. It spent another $5 trillion on the embarrassing and useless war in Afghanistan and got nothing in return. It spent another $14 trillion on the pandemic (i.e. the worldwide overreaction to a flu with a 1% death rate) and got nothing in return. I could go on.

All of this horror *might* be *somewhat* manageable if the USA was booming economically like China was in the early 2000s with double-digit annual GDP growth rates, but the problem is the average annual GDP growth of the USA has been a dreadful 1.5%. Even the most liberal and forgiving economists consider healthy annual GDP growth to be at least 2%, and the USA has been *under that* for *decades*. Canada is just as bad (1.6%) and Europe is even worse with *negative* GDP growth!

With these steroid-like growth rates in spending combined with a stagnant economy, in just a few years 100% of taxes collected by the government will only go to fund the interest on the debt. How is the government going to actually fund government functions when this happens? You tell me. There are several possible scenarios (massive money printing leading to massive inflation, massive borrowing, massive tax increases, etc) and they're all horrible.

Collapse Reason #2. Personal debt has skyrocketed and continues to increase every year.

As bad as government debt is, normal people are just as bad, if not worse. You would have thought that the Global Financial Crisis back in 2008 would have taught people to lay off their debt. Nope. In the USA, total household debt rose from $7.3 trillion in 2003 to $17.6 trillion in Q1 2024, a staggering 139% increase. Credit card balances increased from $692 billion in 2003 to

$1.14 trillion in 2024, a 65% rise. Car loan balances rose from $658 billion in 2003 to $1.62 trillion in 2024, an insane 146% increase. Hilariously, student loan debt (why the hell are people still going to college?) grew from $253 billion in 2003 to $1.6 trillion in 2024, an amazing 533% increase(!).

This is completely unsustainable, especially as the economy gets worse and worse, and the borrowing rates just keep increasing. Just this one statistic alone would be cause enough for an economic collapse, and we've got another 20 to go! And again, many countries are even worse than the USA when it comes to personal debt (like Australia).

Collapse Reason #3. 88% of the entire S&P 500 is owned by just three companies.

BlackRock, State Street, and Vanguard own 88% of the shares of all companies in the S&P 500. This is fascism. If any backwater country in South America or Asia was like this, Americans would make fun of it, but most Americans don't even know that damn near their entire stock market is owned by just three companies. This means corporate control of things like government, media, health care, and real estate.

Worse, this creates a highly fragile and risky system; the entire thing could collapse if any one of these three companies got into trouble (which they will for all of the other reasons I'm listing in this chapter).

This corporate control grows every year and will not stop.

Collapse Reason #4. Human beings in the West are literally dying out. They're not having enough babies to sustain their populations.

A nation needs (approximately) a 2.1 birth replacement rate to maintain its population. 2.1 doesn't *grow* their population. It just *maintains* it. Anything under this number means there are fewer people in that nation every year because more people die than are born. In other words, if your birth replacement rate is under 2.1, your nation and your culture are literally headed for extinction.

With that magic 2.1 number in mind, here are the birth replacement rates of the top ten Western nations listed in order of GDP:

USA: 1.6

Germany: 1.5

UK: 1.7
France: 1.8
Italy: 1.3
Canada: 1.4
Australia: 1.7
Spain: 1.2
Netherlands: 1.6
Switzerland: 1.5

Yeah. Do you see a problem? Do you now see why the left-wing, collapsing governments of most of these nations are allowing millions of third-world immigrants into their nations? It's because it's the only way they can keep GDP and growth rates going. Since Westerners aren't reproducing they have to bring in hordes of poverty-stricken Africans, Muslims, Central Americans, South Americans, and Mexicans into their countries who take up the slack. This then creates a whole new set of problems like increasing crime rates (which we'll cover in a minute), which leads to civil unrest as Westerners protest this (which we'll also cover in a minute) and overloading the already bloated welfare state (creating even more government spending).

It's like a small snowball of problems that gets larger and larger as it rolls down the hill, becoming a massive boulder the size of a city.

Here's a fun fact. Look it up if you don't believe me: no nation or culture in human history has *ever* reversed a below 2.1 replacement rate despite *everything* they tried. 100% of all of them went extinct.

Collapse Reason #5. Westerners get stupider every decade with declining IQs… while Asians get smarter every decade.

From 2006 to 2024, cognitive ability scores (including IQ) dropped across the board, all over the Collapsing West. These cognitive abilities include verbal reasoning, matrix reasoning, reading, and mathematics. IQ scores have been trending downward after decades of increases, with a drop of around 5 IQ points per decade in Western countries. If you think people are stupid now, just wait about 20 years when most people will have IQs of under 100.

However, in Asia (the West's chief economic rival), IQ scores continue to go up every decade with no end in sight.

So who do you think will be in charge of the world 30 or 40 years from now?

Collapse Reason #6. Drug use has skyrocketed in the West over the past 25 years and increases every year as the West gets closer to collapse.

This one is crazy. In the year 2000, 8% of Americans reported using illegal drugs. In 2024 this is now 25% of *all* Americans aged 12 or older, and this is factoring in the fact that more drugs are legal now than they were back in 2000. It's been a steady 3.8% increase year-over-year. Over 50% of Americans (half of all Americans!) have used illicit drugs in their lifetime. The age-adjusted rate of drug overdose deaths has risen more than 14% in several *individual years* since 2018. There were *five times* the amount of drug overdose deaths in 2022 than in 2002 and *double that* from just seven years prior.

The opioid epidemic plus increased use of cocaine, heroin, fentanyl, and psychostimulants like meth, increased stress about the cultural collapse, rising political strife, civil unrest, and worsening economics all contribute to this increased drug use. All of these things are going to get worse over the next 10-20 years, not better, which means more drug usage and more drug deaths.

Collapse Reason #7. Westerners have stopped saving and have no cash left. But Asia is cash-rich and continues to get richer.

Back in 2016, when the economy of the West was much stronger than it is today, I quoted some data in my blogs that reported that 38% of Americans who make more than $100,000 a year could *not* get their hands on $1,000 cash in an emergency. Just think about that for a minute. People considered wealthy Americans don't have a thousand bucks! It also reported that 75% of people making under $50K annually and 67% of people making between $50K and $100K couldn't get their hands on $1K in cash in an emergency.

Savings rates for Americans in the past have usually been around 8-10%, which is considered good. The savings rate today is 2.4%... a 17-year low.

2.4%, that's it. Let's look at some of our Asian friends as a comparison. Malaysia's saving rate is 27%. India's savings rate is 28%. Japan's is 29%. Indonesia and Vietnam are both at 30%. Singapore's is 38%. China's is... get ready for this... 43%.

Hmmmm. The Collapsing West or Rising Asia... gee... who do you think will win in the end? (There's a reason I'm invested in Asia and don't own any American or Western stocks.)

Collapse Reason #8. Westerners' mental health is crumbling before our eyes and gets worse every year.

Only 31% of U.S. adults rated their mental health as "excellent" in 2022, the lowest percentage recorded by Gallup in over two decades. Today in 2024/25, an absolutely staggering 23% of adults (nearly 60 million people) in the USA experienced mental illness in just the past year. Let me say that differently: *one-fourth of the population of the USA is mentally ill.* Isn't that nice?

This is a huge rise in the prevalence of mental health issues across the population. Countries like Canada and the UK are in similar shape. 42% of high school students reported persistent feelings of sadness or hopelessness in the last several years, and this is up from 28% in 2011. Mental health therapists all over the Western world have jam-packed schedules and have trouble taking on new patients, creating an entire industry of huge mental health corporations cashing on this horrible trend.

And this is all getting worse every year, even years after the pandemic has ended.

Collapse Reason #9. Western suicide rates have skyrocketed. Westerners are literally killing themselves more now than ever before, and the rate is increasing.

On top of the massive increase in drug overdose deaths, Westerners are also purposely killing themselves at rates never seen in all of Western history. I remember in the 1980s and 1990s all of us Americans made fun of Japan because of those silly, stressed-out Japanese with their massive suicide rates. Well, guess what? Today, America's suicide rate is now *worse* than Japan's, surpassing Japan's rates in 2022.

Just like in so many other areas, the West has become the very thing the West has always mocked.

Suicide is now the second-leading cause of death for individuals aged 10-24(!). This represents a staggering increase of 52% since the year 2000. Suicide among all ages has risen 40% in the last 20 years. The fastest-rising form of suicide in the USA is people shooting themselves with firearms which accounts for about half of all suicides.

Suicide has become such a huge problem that major social media sites like YouTube have banned the word "suicide" to be spoken or written because they're worried more Westerners might kill themselves if they keep hearing that word (and shit, with all of their mental health problems and drug use, they might be right) forcing people on these platforms to invent entire new silly words and terms like "self erase" or "unalive" (which I'm sure will also be banned soon).

Collapse Reason #10. Westerner's attention spans get worse every year and are now worse than the attention span of a goldfish (yes, literally).

The average attention span has decreased from 12 seconds in 2000 to 8.25 seconds in 2013, making it shorter than that of a goldfish, which is estimated to be around 9 seconds. Using a different type of measurement (attention spans can be measured in several different ways), the average attention span has plummeted from approximately 2.5 minutes in 2004 to just *47 seconds* today, a hilariously horrible 66% decrease over two decades. 59% of Gen Z and Millennials spend more than three hours per day on social media, which contributes significantly to shorter attention spans because social media users frequently switch between tasks and platforms.

I've noticed that when you point out declining attention spans, some people say "So? What's the big deal? Attention spans are shorter, so what?" Here's what shorter attention spans mean for your population:

- Poorer academic performance (Notice how Asians are always the ones winning spelling and math competitions, even when they're held in Western countries?)
- Reduced cognitive development
- Increased stress and anxiety
- Increased ADHD cases
- Decreased work efficiency
- Impaired information retention, gaps in memory
- Inability to focus
- Cultural shift towards instant gratification
- Does any of that shit sound familiar?

Collapse Reason #11. Voters on all sides of the political spectrum in the West have become objectively irrational and can't solve basic problems anymore.

Western countries are democracies (or are supposed to be) and democracies only work as well as the intelligence and objectivity of the voters. Per the above statistics, today you have Western voters who are suicidal, mentally ill, addicted to drugs, getting stupider every year, and have attention spans lower than fish. When you've got people like that selecting your leaders, what kind of leaders are you going to get?

Well, you already know the answer. In Europe, countries like Germany and the UK have been electing leaders that have literally and purposely destroyed their economies and cultures, and in many cases, these leaders get re-elected anyway. The USA has had five completely ridiculous presidents *in a row*:

- Bill Clinton, who was getting blowjobs in the White House, lied under oath numerous times and gave away American nuclear technology to the Chinese. He was re-elected by the voters, by the way.
- George W. Bush, who skyrocketed government spending unlike any other president before him, attacked the wrong country (Iraq) spending trillions on that farce for no reason and started listening to your phone conversations without a warrant. This guy was also re-elected by the voters, by the way.
- Barack Obama, the biggest debt-increasing president in American history, who created a corporatist health care system, started spying on your texts and emails, and presided over *six* different wars. Yes, six. Oh, and he was re-elected by the voters, by the way.
- Donald Trump, the president who increased the debt and deficit faster than any other president in American history *before the pandemic started*, who did literally nothing he promised (build the wall, bring the jobs back, lock her up, kick out the Mexicans, etc) and who was so stupid that in meetings with his staff, he thought Russia owned Finland, didn't know the difference between HPV and HIV, and wanted to shoot nukes at a hurricane. He was eventually re-elected by the voters too.
- Joe Biden, an old man who was so senile that he could barely speak or think coherently for longer than two or three minutes at a time, causing a hidden cabal behind him to secretly run everything while he was president. Nice.

As you can see, this is not about left vs. right, because both sides have become so irrational that they can't vote for leaders who can solve basic problems. People on the left will complain about their high taxes and then turn around and vote for people like Bernie Sanders. People on the right will complain about skyrocketing government spending and debt and then turn around and vote for Trump. And so on.

Look at all the problems I'm listing in this chapter. Now picture the typical left-wing or right-wing Western voter. Based on who this person is and who they support, do you feel they are qualified to solve all of these massive problems? Be honest and as objective as possible, and you know the answer.

By the way, there's a reason that the most prosperous, safest, and well-run countries in the world are *not* democracies as the West understands the term (countries like Singapore, Hong Kong, and my home in Dubai). Food for thought.

Collapse Reason #12. Major banks are collapsing all over the West at rates never seen before in all of Western history.

People have no idea that three of the four biggest bank failures in all of American history happened in 2023. Those would be First Republic Bank, Silicon Valley Bank, and Signature Bank, and these banks were considered some of the more stable banks in the US(!). That's worse than in the Global Financial Crisis of 2008. From 2015 to 2022, there was an average of "only" about 3.6 bank failures per year. In contrast, the year 2023 alone saw a dramatic uptick, with five banks failing within a few months.

Europe's banks are less bad but are still in big trouble. One of the biggest banks in Europe, Switzerland's Credit Suisse, a bank long considered to be one of the most rock-solid in the world, completely collapsed in 2023 and had to be rescued by another big bank (UBS). As I once reported in my blogs, Germany's biggest bank (Germany is the biggest and most important economy in Europe) Deutsche Bank owns more derivatives than *five times* the value of the GDP of the entire Eurozone(!).

Meanwhile, non-Western banks are 100% strong with no major problems. While the USA has 3.6 banks going under every year, the UAE and Qatar have never had a bank failure in their entire history. Japan, even with all of its economic issues, hasn't had *any* in 30 years and Singapore hasn't had any in 40 years. Taiwan is similar except for one blip during the Global Financial Crisis of 2008.

Where would *you* like to put your money for the long term? I know where I'm putting mine.

Collapse Reason #13. Western governments, quickly running out of money, are printing money more now than has ever been printed in all of human history, causing rampant inflation and all kinds of other economic chaos.

Because of stupid voters voting for horrible leaders, Western governments have been spending so much money that they can't raise taxes enough or borrow enough from other countries to keep up with the spending. So instead, they print more dollars, euros, pounds, or whatever to spend which causes more inflation for you and me.

The monetary base of the USA (meaning the total amount of a currency in circulation or held in reserves) was about $600 billion in 1999 and increased to approximately $6 trillion by 2023, reflecting a growth of around 900%(!). The Federal Reserve's balance sheet (which how much money has been printed) was roughly $600 billion in 1999. By late 2023, it had expanded to about $8 trillion, indicating an increase of over 1,200%(!).

During the Global Financial Crisis, the monetary base nearly *doubled* from about $800 billion to over $2 trillion within *just a few months.* Just a few years later we had the pandemic (the worldwide over-reaction to a flu with a 1% death rate) and under Donald Trump, who many Americans consider a Jesus-like savior, they increased the monetary base from around $4 trillion in January 2020 to approximately $9 trillion by October 2021; *that's $5 trillion in new money printing in less than two years(!).*

Europe is in the same death spiral. The European Central Bank (their version of the Federal Reserve) had a balance sheet of around €1 trillion in 1999. By the end of 2023, it had expanded to approximately €8 trillion, an increase of over 700%(!). As just one example, in January 2015, they started printing €60 billion per month, totaling over €3 trillion by the end of 2021. Eurozone government debt levels have also risen dramatically since 1999, from about 60% of GDP to over 90% of GDP by 2023, reflecting increased borrowing facilitated by, you guessed it, printing more money.

If you've noticed that things like health care, groceries, gasoline, real estate, and other basics have become much more expensive lately, this is why. Your insane, suicidal Western government, controlled by horrible leaders voted in by stupid voters, is constantly printing up trillions of dollars/euros/pounds which makes everything you buy with these currencies more expensive. In the

US alone, the inflation rate was about 1.6% in 2016. By 2022, it had surged to over 7%, marking the highest levels of inflation *in four decades.*

This money-printing thing alone will destroy the West because they simply won't stop doing it until they're all bankrupt.

Collapse Reason #14. Western school absenteeism has skyrocketed and continues to rise.

According to the USA National Center for Education Statistics, here are the rates of high school absenteeism in the past 25 years:

- 2000: 5.0%
- 2015: 6.1%
- 2020: 11.1%
- 2024: 22%

Notice a trend? True, there was a spike during the pandemic (the worldwide overreaction to a flu with a 1% death rate) but it's still been trending upwards and continues to do so long after the pandemic ended. This is bad because we know for a statistical fact that students who miss 10% of the school year (approximately 18 days), which is how "absenteeism" is normally defined, are significantly more likely to struggle academically and eventually drop out.

This is also cutting across all socioeconomic levels. For example, Connecticut is one of the richest states in the USA but more than 22% of its current high school students have either dropped out or have high absentee rates, and more than 25% are flunking out of all of their classes.

Collapse Reason #15. Real unemployment rates are at historically high levels and aren't getting any better.

Before I give you these government stats, you need to understand that any unemployment numbers from the government are always underreported. The real unemployment rate is always worse than what they report for several reasons, some of which I'll explain in a minute. So whatever these numbers are, mentally increase them at least a little bit. Secondly, most economists and government experts (ahem) consider a "good" unemployment rate to be 4%-6%. Keep all of this in mind.

First, we had the Global Financial Crisis (2007-08), and the Great Recession lasting to 2011 or so. The unemployment rate in the USA surged from (again, these are government numbers) 5.0% in December 2007 to a peak of 10.0% in October 2009 due to the financial crisis, one of the most significant increases in modern history. Long-term unemployed (those out of work for 27 weeks or more) peaked at an insane 48% in April 2010. (This is a little image of what is to come soon.)

Then we had the pandemic (the worldwide overreaction to a flu with a 1% death rate, and another little image of what is to come) where the unemployment rate hit 14.8% in April 2020.

As of the writing of this book, the *reported* USA unemployment rate is 4.4%, but this is a meaningless figure. The real picture is painted by the U-6 unemployment rate which includes people who can't find jobs and thus give up looking, plus people who want full-time jobs but can't get them and are stuck with low-paying part-time jobs. *That* rate is 8.8%. Plus none of these numbers include older people who really want to work but couldn't find a job so they retired early instead, usually in a state of poverty. So if you factor in the normal employment rate, the U-6 rate, old people who can't find work, and the shenanigans governments use to fudge these numbers, the *real* unemployment rate is well over 15%... much worse than the "good" rate of 4%-6%. And this shows signs of getting worse over time, not better. We'll talk more about this in the AI chapters of this book.

But it gets even *worse*. At the moment, there are currently around seven million able-bodied men in the USA between the ages of 25-55 who are not only unemployed, but who are not looking for jobs at all, preferring to stay at home, play video games, watch TV, and smoke weed. The USA has *never* had *anything* like this in all of its history, in terms of real numbers or percentages.

And again, this gets worse every year.

Collapse Reason #16. Homelessness is steadily increasing all over the Western world, and in many regions, it's skyrocketing.

There are numerous stats on this but they vary from region to region. Regions like Germany and California have entire sections of cities overrun with homeless people, often drug addicts. Feel free to do your own research, but all the stats show that homelessness is on the rise all over the Collapsing Trifecta. There are double-digit increases year-over-year in many parts of the USA. France and Germany's homelessness has *more than doubled* in the past 25 years and in Canada it has almost doubled.

Not a great trend, and it's getting worse.

Collapse Reason #17. The rate of single-parent fatherless families is at world-wide historic highs in the West and keeps getting worse every year.

If you're a more left-wing person, you might not consider fatherlessness a major problem for society. Well, sorry, but the facts are very clear on this. Fatherless kids are:

- 10 times more likely to abuse drugs or alcohol
- 11 times more likely to exhibit violent behavior
- 20 times more likely to be incarcerated
- 63% of youth suicides
- 85% of children exhibiting behavioral disorders
- 71% of high school dropouts
- 90% of all homeless and runaway children

It doesn't matter how left-wing you are or how much you love single mothers (I think single moms are great!). The objective reality is that fatherlessness is absolutely horrible for your nation's culture and economic future.

Now let's look at the stats. The USA has the highest rate of children living in a single-parent household of any nation in the entire world. In the USA approximately 23% of children are living with one parent and no other adults. This is over *three times the world average* of 7% of children raised by one parent.

It's not just the USA. This is a serious and growing problem all over the Western world. Fatherlessness in the UK, New Zealand, and Australia is at 15% and rising. Scandinavia's at 17%. Canada's is 19% and France's fatherlessness rate is 20%.

In most of the Western world, the average school-age boy only spends about 30 minutes per week in one-on-one conversations with his dad. For comparison, the same boy on average will spend around 44 hours a week watching TV, the internet, or playing video games.

And as always, these rates are getting worse as time goes on, not better.

Let's compare Asian countries to these collapsing Western nations. While international stats vary, the fatherlessness rates of China, Japan, India, Hong Kong, and Vietnam are all well below 10%.

Collapse Reason #18. Westerners pay the highest tax rates in the entire world, by far, even though infrastructure in the West worsens every year.

As I've analyzed on my blogs, the typical American, if you add up all the taxes he pays in state taxes, federal taxes, payroll taxes, property taxes (even if he rents his home and doesn't own it), sales taxes, and pass-through corporate taxes and excise taxes, pays a whopping 51% to 70% of his entire income in some form of tax to the collapsing United States government. These represent taxes you see (like what your employer takes from your paycheck on your paystub) to taxes you don't see (like when you fill your gas tank and pay for gas; a lot of that is tax, not gas). This nice, honorable government uses these funds to do things like bomb countries that have never attacked you, give trillions of dollars to people who could work but don't want to, and bail out multimillionaire bankers and hedge fund managers.

There are many cities in Canada and Europe where average people pay 70% in total taxes to their collapsing, corrupt, quasi-socialist, quasi-corporatist governments.

On top of that, infrastructure in these countries is crumbling before our very eyes. If you paid the highest taxes in the world but had the best infrastructure in the world, I guess that would be one thing. But it's now common for Western cities to have streets with potholes that never get fixed, bridges and buildings that collapse, water and electrical systems that are 50+ years old, and so on.

Westerners don't realize that *this doesn't happen in other countries.* Hong Kong had a 15% flat tax for decades and became the greatest economy in the world (before 2019 or so when China cracked down on it). I live in Dubai in the United Arab Emirates, which has no income tax, no property taxes, no payroll taxes, no capital gains taxes, and the smallest corporate tax in the world, and it's literally and objectively one of the best places to live with the best infrastructure on the planet. I also spend several months a year in Paraguay which has a tiny personal income tax rate of around 10% and a corporate tax that's the same, but even better, because it's a territorial tax country, any income you receive in Paraguay from outside of the country *isn't taxed at all.* You can make $10 million a year in Paraguay and if all that income comes from outside of Paraguay, you will pay *zero taxes.*

Because of all this, I pay a tiny fraction of my income in taxes compared to normal Westerners. I know people who pay zero taxes or very close to it, 100% legally, because they simply don't live in the Collapsing West.

But if you still live in the Collapsing West, you're getting raped. You're *literally* paying the highest tax rates in the world for crappy infrastructure. It's just stupid.

Collapse Reason #19. Crime rates and civil unrest are increasing all over the West.

I've done several YouTube videos breaking down the exact numbers on this, and you're more than willing to take a look at those if you'd like. The bottom line is that crime rates in the West have risen so much in recent years that cities all over the United States, Canada, and Western Europe are now experiencing crime rates on par with some of the most dangerous cities in Africa. Again, if you don't believe me, go look it up yourself and I think you'll be shocked. I certainly was.

Worse, in many of these cities, including London, Los Angeles, and Paris, the police aren't even bothering to arrest criminals. Many of these places have made crimes such as shoplifting de facto legal.

To speak anecdotally, I've lived in Dubai for four years and have never witnessed a crime here (because of its effectively 0% crime rate) yet during those same four years when I visited the UK and the USA on brief visits, I witnessed crimes happening right before my eyes, including theft.

On top of increasing crime rates, you have also increasing *civil unrest*, as in riots and protests, which have skyrocketed all over the Collapsing West (as I predicted it would way back in 2014 when I wrote about this in the first edition of The Unchained Man). Civil unrest in the UK and USA has *doubled* over the past decade. The Allianz Risk Barometer shows the top risks for businesses, and for the first time they are now showing "civil unrest" as the *eighth* highest risk to any business operating in the Western world. This has never happened before in all of Western history.

Today, you are literally safer living in most parts of Latin America than you are in most major cities in the USA or Western Europe. No one ever thought that would ever happen, but it has.

And it gets worse every year.

Collapse Reason #20. Less countries are using the US Dollar and are moving away from it.

The backbone of not just the USA but of most of the Western world is the US Dollar. It's the primary reason why the USA has de facto dominated most of the planet since the end of World War II. But now, countries are abandoning the dollar and using other currencies instead.

Worldwide US Dollar reserve currency usage is down from 71% in the year 2000 to just 51% today. There's been a 5.5X increase in non-traditional (i.e. non-dollar) use of currencies worldwide.

Here's a fun stat. In the year 2000, 80% of countries traded more with the US than with China. Today, this has flipped; now 75% of the world's countries trade more with China than the US. Yikes.

Many people have said that the US Dollar is going to collapse "soon." I do not agree with this analysis because the data doesn't indicate this. The dollar is still quite important and quite entrenched in world economics and will be for a long time. However, what *is* true is that the dollar is absolutely getting weaker every year that goes by, and in your lifetime you *will* see the dollar replaced by something else. None of this is good for America or the rest of the Collapsing West.

Collapse Reason #21. In the Western world, the poverty rate is increasing while the middle class is decreasing.

This is one of those stats that would be reason enough for Western collapse even if nothing else was wrong. When your middle class gets smaller every year, your society is in huge trouble no matter what else is happening.

In 2000, the US poverty rate was around 11.1%, which is frankly pretty bad for a country as financially successful as the USA. By 2023, it had *increased* to 12.8%. Increased? Wait a minute. The poverty rate in your country should be *declining* every year, not getting *higher*. That's indicative of a future collapse. I live in countries where the poverty rate gets smaller every year, which is how a country is supposed to function.

The middle class is also in trouble in the West. The share of adults living in middle-class households has decreased significantly, from 61% in 1971 to 50% in 2021. Since 2000, real wages for middle-class workers have stagnated or declined, with many workers experiencing little to no wage growth when adjusted for inflation.

In the year 2000, about 50% of children born into the lowest income quintile (meaning the lowest one-fifth) moved up to a higher quintile by adulthood. By 2022, this figure had dropped to approximately 40% and keeps getting worse. *This is really bad.* It's even worse than the increasing poverty rate since the middle class is the backbone of any economy. A declining middle class means a declining country.

Chapter 4

What Will Western Collapse Look Like?

When I discuss these topics, these are the top two questions I receive:

1. When exactly will the collapse occur?
2. What exactly do you mean by "collapse?" and/or What exactly will happen when the collapse occurs?

I already answered question number one back in Chapter 2. The summary is that we don't know exactly when it will happen (anywhere from 2-25 years, but even that is a guess) but the odds are overwhelming that it will happen in your lifetime, meaning it doesn't matter when it will happen; you need to address it right now before it happens and negatively affects you and your loved ones.

In this chapter, I will address the second question, what the Creeping Darkness will look like and what Westerners will experience when the Western world collapses.

The reality is that the word "collapse" is somewhat broad and can mean several different things.

When the word "collapse" is heard, most people assume that means the United States, Canada, Europe, and/or other Western regions suddenly turn into something that looks like a Mad Max movie where masses of starving people are looking for scraps to eat in the streets while bands of heavily armed zombies or murderous marauders are slaughtering people left and right and stealing everyone's food, water, gold, bullets, and women. Because of this assumption, many of these people just snort and blow this all off as some kind of ridiculous fantasy. Other people take this 100% seriously and start building fully-stocked underground bomb shelters in their backyards.

Both of these types of people are being irrational and silly. While I agree the Mad Max scenario is possible, it is extremely unlikely and I've been saying that for over 15 years. However, just because "collapse" doesn't mean Mad Max it doesn't mean many horrible things won't happen to millions of innocent people. This means that while building a survival bunker is a tad ridiculous, doing absolutely nothing whatsoever to prepare for the Creeping Darkness because you think this is all bullshit is equally ridiculous.

The collapse of the Western world probably won't be Mad Max. Instead, it will be one of five possible collapse scenarios. While some of these are worse than others, all of them are bad. I will describe each one of them right now.

Which one of these five scenarios will it be? Once again, I don't know, you don't know, and none of the experts know for sure. To repeat what I already said, anyone who says they know exactly what the collapse of the West will look like is either irrational, lying, or trying to sell you something. **We don't know exactly what will happen and there is no way to know. All we know is likely one of these collapse scenarios will occur.**

Since we don't know which of these scenarios it will be, all we can do is come up with a battle plan comprehensive enough to protect us *from all five possible scenarios*. We'll discuss exactly how to do that in upcoming chapters.

The Five Western Collapse Scenarios

Collapse Scenario #1: Secession or Balkanization

In this scenario, certain groups of Westerners wise up and secede from their greater, collapsing parasite countries. This means states in the USA secede from the union and declare independence, and/or European countries break away from the EU and go back to their currencies, and/or provinces in Canada or European nations break away from their host countries.

A "light" example of this would be Hungary exiting the EU, similar to what the UK did a few years ago. Heavier examples of this would be scenarios like Scotland seceding from the UK, Catalonia seceding from Spain, Texas seceding from the USA, or Quebec seceding from Canada.

The larger countries that remain will still collapse, and the smaller break-away countries might, and I mean *might* have a chance at doing okay, or at least less badly, if they embrace intelligent economic policies. Sadly, due to modern-day left-wing and right-wing big-government cultural factors, most of them probably won't do this and will simply collapse anyway.

I consider succession as possible but unlikely. As shown by places that talk a big secession game but never actually do it (Scotland, Quebec, Texas, etc) modern-day low-testosterone Westerners just don't have the balls to actually break away from their respective big governments, cutting off the flow of welfare cash and possibly inciting a civil war. So in my view, succession is a nice idea, but somewhat unlikely in the modern era where Westerners, including right-wing ones, worship at the altar of big government even if they complain about it occasionally.

All that being said, there is one extreme type of secession which is called *balkanization* which is quite different. This is when a larger Western nation or economy gets so bad that instead of having one state or province break away, the entire country breaks apart into a large number of tiny independent nations. Examples of this were during the 1990s when Yugoslavia broke up into seven nations and the Soviet Union broke up into 14.

Balkanization is the least bad of all the collapse scenarios by far. The reason is that, no matter how poorly managed most of those little countries likely will be, statistically speaking at least *some* of these little countries will actually do the right thing and adopt sane and effective economic and monetary policies. We saw this with the ex-Soviet nations. Some of these countries made a lot of correct decisions and did reasonably well (like Georgia and Estonia) and some made poor decisions and languished (like Belarus and Tajikistan).

I've said for years that the only way you can "save" the United States of America at this point is to a line down the middle of the country, then draw four horizontal lines across the country, thereby creating ten small, long, horizontal nations, each one with a port city (which is critical). Split off Alaska and Hawaii, and now instead of one bloated, collapsing, cluster-fuck empire, you have 12 small nations that can set their own laws and path. Most of these nations will be just as quasi-socialist and quasi-corporatist as the original United Sates, but the odds are at least one or two of them would embrace free market capitalism, property rights, rule of law, Austrian economics, low taxes, and zero or near-zero money printing.

The problem with balkanization is that while it might sound cool to objective observers like myself, things like this only occur after the people of that country go through a long, prolonged period of economic chaos and horror. So balkanization is not something you want to experience yourself. Instead, you want to move away from your collapsing nation, then if it ever balkanizes, you can move back to one of the smaller countries committed to doing things right. If the USA ever balkanizes in the future, once the bloodbath and madness are over, I'd be happy to move back to one of the smaller nations if they embraced hardcore libertarian policies… but until and unless that day happens, I'm not living in the USA and staying as far away from it as I can, thank you very much.

Collapse Scenario #2: Slow Decline Into Irrelevance

People are often surprised to learn that 400 years ago, Portugal ruled the world. Back then, it was a major superpower. Even distant nations in Asia feared them and kissed their asses. Today, Portugal is a ridiculous, tiny, bankrupt country that barely appears on a world map and that the IMF keeps having to bail out just to keep alive.

In this scenario, this is what happens to the West. There's no major event or collapse that wipes everything out or screws everything up. Instead, every year the countries in the Collapsing Trifecta get smaller, weaker, stupider, poorer, and more indebted. For example, in several decades, the USA and/or Europe is a small country or region a fraction of its current size, surrounded by large Asian, Muslim, and/or Hispanic-dominated nations.

This scenario is less traumatic than the others because it happens more slowly. The problem is this collapse scenario, like succession, is quite unlikely. I just showed you all the reasons in the prior chapter why the Collapsing USA, Cuckoo Canada, and Suicidal Europe don't have many decades left of life. Over the next 30 years at the very most, many of these nations will likely collapse under one of the other collapse scenarios I outline in this chapter.

I've noticed there is a certain group of people who assume that Slow Decline Into Irrelevance is the most likely collapse scenario. "Yeah," they say, "The USA/Canada/Europe will collapse eventually but it will probably take 100 years or something, so no need to freak out about it." I'm sorry, but while I agree this is *possible*, collapse at that long of a time frame is *extremely* unlikely. If you don't believe that, I suggest you re-read Chapter 3.

The collapse will (likely) occur much faster than most people think.

Collapse Scenario #3: Currency Crisis

This is the scenario that I consider to be the most likely of all the collapse scenarios, by far. This is what all the data and trends are pointing at.

In this scenario, the US dollar and/or the Euro hyperinflates or hyperdeflates, ruining jobs and businesses all across the Western world and destroying personal wealth on a mass scale.

In a hyperinflation scenario, major nations like China, Japan, Brazil, Saudi Arabia, and/or others stop borrowing money from the USA. Trillions of US dollars suddenly flood back into the US, crashing the value of the dollar and turning the United States into the 1920's Weimar Republic or something similar. A loaf of bread then costs $300 and all of your savings, investments, and real estate are suddenly worthless. (On the other hand, certain assets like precious metals and possibly cryptocurrency skyrocket in value and make a small percentage of the population very rich.)

In a hyperdeflation scenario, some major catastrophe occurs somewhere in the world, like Europe collapsing, a major Asian or European war, or a nuclear exchange. In a panic, the world stupidly flees to the US dollar, thinking it's safe. Or, everything is fine in the world but the US stock market bubble finally bursts and the government can no longer print its way out of it.

Regardless of the cause, the stock market crashes by at least 75% and many commodities, including precious metals, crash similarly. What remains of the US and European manufacturing sector gets completely wiped out. Banks call in all of their debts and no one can pay them, creating a scenario like the 1980s Savings and Loan Crisis, only 100 times worse, with everyone losing their homes and cars. Everyone is screwed. (On the other hand, people with zero debt who own vast amounts of liquid dollars might do very well if they quickly buy everything in sight and get very rich a few years later once they escape to non-Western countries.)

I already showed you the statistics back in Chapter 3 why Currency Crisis is the most likely collapse scenario. It could be hyperinflation or hyperdeflation, and once again, we don't know which one it could be (though I consider hyperinflation to be more likely).

Unfortunately, the collapse scenario that is the most likely is also one of the worst ones. This is simply the result of Western governments constantly "kicking the can down the road" since the 1970s, pushing systemic economic problems into the future instead of fixing them.

Collapse Scenario #4: Totalitarianism

In this scenario, the economy, crime, and/or the culture eventually gets so bad that people freak out and irrationally embrace a strongman (or strongwoman) authoritarian who takes power in a major nation or nations, such as in the USA, UK, France, or Germany, along with many other people who support him or her in the legislative bodies of said nation. An actual coup d'état is also possible.

It doesn't matter if the new authoritarian leader is a left-winger or right-winger (statistically, it's a 50/50 toss-up as to which one you'll get). The result ends up being the same. Sweeping, authoritarian changes are enacted. Personal and business bank accounts, retirement accounts, and other assets are seized for the "good of the nation" (under a right-wing authoritarian) or the "good of the people" (under a left-wing authoritarian).

Free speech is revoked "temporarily," which is a lie. Foreigners or domestic political opponents are blamed for everything and are expelled or imprisoned. Travel outside of the country is limited, making citizens unable to leave their dying nation unless they hold foreign passports. A nationwide content-blocking internet firewall like China's is put in place. War is also very likely. Personal freedom, as Westerners currently understand it, completely vanishes.

A lot of left-wingers these days fear this scenario with the rise of right-wing populist figures in the past several years like Trump in the USA, Bolsonario in Brazil, Modi in India, Putin in Russia, Orbán in Hungary, or Bukele in El Salvador. As usual, this fear is based on emotions and not fact. While I consider the Totalitarianism collapse scenario as more likely than Secession or Slow Decline Into Irrelevance, I don't consider it very likely and consider it far less likely than a Currency Crisis.

Also, these left-wingers could easily experience a *left-wing* authoritarian ruler just as easily as a right-wing one who would be just as bad. I agree an authoritarian USA under a dictator-for-life Donald Trump would be very bad and I would never live in a country like that, but a Hillary Clinton, Kamala Harris, or Angela Merkel-like dictator would be just as bad.

Regardless of my doubts about Totalitarianism actually happening, I have to acknowledge Totalitarianism is a real possibility since historically it has happened in many Western nations many times when things got bad enough. And things are going to get bad. So while I don't consider this the most likely outcome, I wouldn't be surprised if it happened.

Collapse Scenario #5: War and/or Large-Scale Terrorism

I published an article on one of my blogs in March of 2016. Here's the exact quote I said in that article regarding one of the war scenarios I said was distinctly possible in a few years: *"Putin finally crosses a line of no return and causes a major war between Russia and a European nation(s), forcing China and/or the US to get involved"* Unfortunately, I was right. Just a few years later he invaded Ukraine, and now the USA, China, and many other nations are directly involved, just as I predicted. As of the writing of this book, the outcome of this conflict and its specific effect on Western collapse is unclear, but it certainly doesn't look like it will be *good* for the West.

This collapse scenario is broken down into two possible scenarios.

The first scenario is War. The War collapse scenario means that somewhere in the world, two or more major nations (Western or non-Western) attack each other and force various Western nations, already in a state of collapse, to get involved either militarily or financially. Things escalate like dominos, very similar to World War I, and things get bad enough that one or more Western nations collapse under the weight of what occurs.

Right now we have many possible flashpoint catalysts for this scenario:

- Russia vs. Ukraine
- Russia vs. NATO
- Russia vs. Georgia
- Israel vs. Hamas
- Israel vs. Lebanon
- Israel vs. Iran
- Iran vs. Saudi Arabia
- China vs. Taiwan
- China vs. Japan
- China vs. India
- China vs. United States
- United States vs. Venezuela
- United States vs. North Korea
- North Korea vs. South Korea
- Turkey vs. Greece
- Turkey vs. Syria
- India vs. Pakistan
- Armenia vs. Azerbaijan
- Serbia vs. Kosovo

Moreover, I haven't even listed the possibility of *civil* war in many countries, including many Western ones, so add that to the list as well.

If any one of these matches light too close to the gasoline, the collapse of many Western nations, already economically and culturally fragile, could be triggered.

It's important to note here that a War collapse scenario doesn't mean a Western nation like the USA is defeated militarily. Many Americans believe America is 100% safe from defeat in a war because of America's unrivaled military power. This is factually incorrect, but not for the reasons they think. The financial state of the USA is so precarious that a major war right now or in the future could cause a *financial* collapse for the USA (or the UK, Germany, etc) far before a military defeat or victory takes place. Go look at what happened to the Roman Empire for more details on how this could easily happen.

The second possible scenario here is Large-Scale Terrorism. This is just like the war scenario except that the catalyst isn't a war but instead a terrorist attack (or similar) where a lot of people die and/or lose trillions of dollars.

The attacked country goes insane and kills millions of people in response, launching one or more wars that initiate an economic collapse.

You've already seen this happen. In 2001, terrorists killed just under 3,000 Americans. Then America lost its fucking mind and spent the next 20 years launching wars against seven different countries, spent over 20 trillion dollars of taxpayer money, and murdered literally millions of people, the vast majority of whom were innocent civilians who had nothing to do with any of this. You're seeing a similar scenario on a smaller scale play out in Israel right now, and you can see how angry that makes Westerners on both political sides even though most of them don't live in Israel, have never even been there, and know almost nothing about it.

If this happens in the future, it won't be planes flying into buildings or paragliders dropping homemade bombs. Instead, it will be one of these scenarios:

- Drone strikes
- Cyberterrorism
- Bioterrorism (even if it's by accident like what happened with COVID-19)
- Infrastructure-based terrorism (like taking out the electricity of a major city for a month or longer)
- Coordinated sniper attacks (like the DC Sniper about 15 years ago)
- Dirty bomb
- Small nuclear bomb (not a nuclear missile, but a nuclear bomb smuggled in via a ship, train, or van)

I'm a pacifist and I'm against the initiation of force used against anyone for any reason, which means I'm 100% opposed to literally all forms of terrorism. But regardless of my personal opinions, based on how goddamn overreactive we've seen Americans, Israelis, Russians, and Eastern Europeans get when they're attacked, any one of these terrorism scenarios could easily set off a chain of events that leads to war which then leads to Western collapse, even if the military of the Western side is more powerful.

Is The Collapse 100% Guaranteed?

Nothing in life is guaranteed. Anything is possible. Is it *possible* that nothing bad will happen and that America, Canada, Europe, etc will be just fine over the next several decades? I'm rational and objective, so of course I have to state for the record that this is indeed possible.

However, as in all things in life, you need to remove yourself from the word "possible" and instead focus on the word "probable." It's *possible* that the Western world won't collapse at all and everything will be fine for the rest of your life, just like it's *possible* you could win $10 million in the lottery next week.

But I wouldn't bet on either of these things because they're not *probable*.

So change the collapse of the Western world from "guaranteed" to "overwhelmingly likely" and now we're back in reality. The odds are overwhelming that the collapse of the Western world will occur in your lifetime no matter what you do (more on this in the next chapter). This means you're foolish if you just sit around and live your life like you always have, making no major changes or corrections, and assuming your collapsing Western country will be just fine forever.

To be fair, there is one thing that could avert Western collapse. That is someone could invent something that currently doesn't exist, and this new thing is so revolutionary that it completely and radically changes the entire human condition, enough that it completely saves the West from all of the problems I've outlined in this book.

A possible example, and I'm just spitballing here, is that someone invents a battery the size of a vitamin pill that costs five dollars and can power your entire house for 100 years with zero environmental waste. Or someone invents a cheap, portable machine that can instantly 3D print cheeseburgers out of thin air for a cost of a couple of pennies, that tastes fantastic, has only 200 calories, is packed with vitamins and protein, and has no flour, sugar, seed oils, or trans fats.

I admit that amazing inventions like this could change the status quo enough to possibly avert Western collapse. Maybe.

There are two big problems with this, however:

1. How do you know for sure someone is going to invent something like this? How do you know it will be invented fast enough, well before the collapse? How do you know the inventor's government will even allow it, or not suppress it, or make it illegal? How do you know it will be cheap enough for you to get access to it quickly?
2. More importantly, there is nothing you can personally do to ensure something like this will be invented. You can't vote something like this into existence, so there are no political solutions available to you. It's literally and completely out of your control. All you can do is sit back like a powerless pussy and just "hope" that someone somewhere will do this and save you. Does that sound like a good plan to save you and your family?

Even if the possibility exists of something like this occurring, do you really want to bet your entire life, finances, well-being, and future on it? I certainly don't! I'd rather take steps to protect myself. That way I don't need to constantly worry and hope that someone will invent something that will solve all of my problems. I'll be happy no matter what happens, whether or not the West is saved.

"But what about AI? This one AI expert said that AI will save all of us and make the world into a utopia!"

Oh, don't worry, I'm going to address that exact topic in great detail in Chapter 6 when I talk about the second part of the Creeping Darkness, the AI Black Hole of Unknown. Hint: it's not going to be pretty.

Chapter 5

Why There Is Literally Nothing You Can Do To Stop Western Collapse

The biggest challenge with the Creeping Darkness is that most Westerners either don't know it's coming, think it will be mild if it does, or think it won't happen until long past they're dead.

Because you're reading this book you're likely not deeply entrenched in any of those categories. The problem is that the odds are pretty good that you are in the second biggest group of people that I mentioned back in Chapter 2. These are folks who think the collapse of the West, USA, Canada, UK, or whatever can be prevented via political, social, or cultural means.

These are people who understand the West is going to collapse but if we just elect this one guy to high office, he'll prevent it, and then we'll all be okay. Or if we just get this one political party in power, or get X amount of people in our country to convert to this one religion, or if we pass this one big law in our government, then, yay, we've won, and now none of us need to worry about Western collapse anymore and we can just get on with our lives.

It's a nice thought. It really is. It's comforting because it gives humans what they emotionally crave: a purpose, something to do, and an enemy to fight (those oh-so-evil people on the other side of the political spectrum). The problem is that it's factually inaccurate. As I clearly showed through the over 100 statistics in Chapter 3 (and those weren't all the statics I could have shown; there's a lot more) the West is in such bad shape from over 20 different angles that preventing the collapse via political or social means is now literally impossible.

Back in the early to mid-1990s, before the collapse began in earnest, there may have been certain governmental policies or cultural initiatives that could have been enacted to prevent the collapse. I remember voting for Ross Perot back in the early 1990s and saw how exciting it was when he got 19% of the popular vote even though he wasn't a Democrat or a Republican. Even back then, Americans knew the two-party political system was bullshit. But then the elites stepped in, made some changes in the electoral process, and now no third party can ever make that kind of splash ever again. The Democrats and Republicans (and the non-American equivalents in your country if you don't live in the USA) jammed the accelerator down on Western collapse in the early 2000s, voters became even more insane, and now here we are, far past the window of opportunity to save the West.

Today:

- There is no person you can elect to high office who can prevent Western collapse.
- There is no political party you can put into power that can prevent Western collapse.
- There is no new law or set of laws you can enact or repeal that can prevent Western collapse.
- There are no governmental reforms you can enact that can prevent Western collapse.
- There is no international organization you can support that can prevent Western collapse.
- There is no political protest you can engage in that can prevent Western collapse.
- There is no boycott you can engage in that can prevent Western collapse.
- There is no religion or political ideology you can embrace or encourage others to embrace that can prevent Western collapse.
- There is no social movement you can form or join that can prevent Western collapse.
- There are no arguments you can convince people of, in person or on social media, that can prevent Western collapse.

It is mathematically impossible to financially save the Western world at this point, particularly the economies of the Collapsing Trifecta. It is also physically impossible to completely and radically change the deep-seated Societal Programming of over 720 million people (the total population of the West) to turn things around.

I know that your irrational emotions are screaming right now that what I'm saying isn't true, that if we just defeat the fucking so-and-sos and/or get so-and-so into office as President or Prime Minister, then we can, as the Trump supporters used to say, make our country great again. Again, this is all emotion on your part with no facts, data, rationality, or objectivity. It's all a false fantasy in the 2020s and 2030s.

If, by the time you get to Part Two in this book, you still irrationally believe, even a little, that voting, protesting, arguing with people on the internet, writing your congressman, trying to get people to convert to a certain religion or any other social change can save your collapsing Western country, then you are far less likely to take the actions necessary to save yourself and your loved ones once we get to the how-to techniques in this book. You'll read those techniques and think, "Wow, those are really cool," and then do nothing except vote in the next rigged election, and then when the Creeping Darkness and the AI Black Hole of Unknown come to your home, you'll be wiped out (literally or figuratively) just like everyone else.

The Excuse-Makers

There's a common subcategory of these "if we just do this one social thing we can prevent collapse" people. These are people who say this:

"Well, yeah, okay, you're right, no matter who we vote for in the next election, our Western country will collapse and there's nothing we can do to stop it. But! If we elect Person A to run our country, the collapse will happen slower than if we elect Person B. Person B is a total nutjob and will accelerate the collapse! So we all need to get out there and vote for Person A!!!"

There are millions of these people, all over the internet and in many different countries. I encounter them all the time when I discuss Western collapse.

What they're really saying is, "Vote for Person A! He'll destroy our country slower than Person B!" Wow, what a great campaign slogan. This is how completely psychotic politics has become in the modern era. Westerners in the 1980s would never say anything this insane, but this is now almost the norm today.

There are several problems with this viewpoint above and beyond the fact that it's completely nonsensical.

The first problem is that some of these people assume the Western collapse scenario will be scenario #2 in the prior chapter, Slow Decline Into Irrelevance. The only way to make their irrational excuse work is to assume that their collapsing Western country will be just fine for a very long time, and be fine even longer if they elect Person A.

Here's an example I've seen stated by these people. "If we elect Kamala Harris, America will collapse in 75 years. But if we elect Trump instead, it will collapse in 100 years. Hey man, 25 years is a long time! That's a big difference!"

The problem is that the USA doesn't have 75 years or 100 years. As I've been saying throughout this book, the collapse of America (and other countries in the Collapsing Trifecta) will happen *in your lifetime*. In your lifetime isn't 75 or 100 years from now. It's 10 years from now, 20 years from now, perhaps

30 years from now. If your country collapses in your lifetime, which it will, then it doesn't matter exactly when it will collapse, as I clearly spelled out back in Chapter 1. A collapse in 10 years versus a collapse in 16 years doesn't matter, you need to take action to protect yourself now. I explained this with the seatbelt analogy, and these excuse-makers are quintessential examples of people who just don't want to wear their seatbelts and are trying to weasel their way around doing that.

So what they are *really* saying is, "If we elect Person A, maybe I *won't* have to leave my country or set up an international backup plan or start my own business! Cool!"

Sorry. Incorrect.

The second problem is that most of these excuse-makers are just lying. Here's how I know. For the past few months, whenever a person on the internet or in real life makes this excuse about voting for Person A to potentially extend *but not prevent* the collapse, I will respond, "Great. So when are you leaving your country then?" If you vote for Trump (or whomever else is your current Person A, because he's not the only one) since you know that even if that person gets elected your country will still collapse, then obviously you should be making plans to permanently move out of your collapsing nation right now as well. You should vote for Trump and then immediately make plans to leave the USA forever. If you're not making plans to do so, then what the hell are you doing? You just said that your country is going to collapse even if you elect Person A, so why would you stay there just because Person A is in power for a few years?

100% of the time I have asked these excuse-makers when they are leaving their collapsing countries, they either don't answer the question or change the subject. In other words, they're just full of shit. They're saying that their country will collapse under the Person A they support but they really think that it won't, or might not.

So next time you think that excuse yourself (or are about to say it or type it), stop, pause, and think very carefully. Once you're done voting for Person A what exactly are your plans for leaving your collapsing country?

If the answer is none, then you're being dishonest or irrational.

Chapter 6

The AI Black Hole of Unknown

One of my favorite movies when I was a little kid in the early 1980s was The Black Hole. It showed a gigantic, blue-black swirling mass that sucked everything into it. For years, most people thought that's what real black holes looked like. A few decades later, science proved us all wrong, and the correct appearance of what a black hole really looks like was featured in the movie Interstellar. Instead of a swirling hole in space, black holes look like a gigantic black sphere with a yellow halo and a yellow ring cutting across the front of it. Not quite as cool looking as the 80s movie, but still intimidating.

Today you can look at shortform videos of what a real black hole would look like if it was right next to the Earth. Honestly, these videos are disturbing. You're walking outside on a bright sunny day, look up, and suddenly see this gigantic black hole blotting out most of the sky, sucking everything into it.

This is the perfect metaphor for the next part of the Creeping Darkness: the AI Black Hole of Unknown.

I'm sure you've heard more than you can stand all about the excitement, fear, concern, interest, capital, and expansion of artificial intelligence (AI) in our lives and companies, both large and small. I use AI tools daily and likely you are using one or more of these tools yourself, or are at least aware of their commonalty. You've also seen how fast this technology is advancing, faster than TV in the 1950s, faster than computers in the 1970s or 1980s, faster than the internet in the 1990s or 2000s, and even faster than social media and smartphones in the 2000s. Every three or four months there is an entirely new revolution, power, or feature AI can do.

Whether we like it or not or want it or not, AI is coming to your life in a very big way, and very soon; probably sooner than you think.

There are three distinct schools of thought about this.

The first group of people are those who think AI is wonderful and will always be wonderful. AI makes our lives better. AI will improve our productivity, possibly so much that it will avert Western collapse! AI will make medical breakthroughs to eliminate cancer, heart attacks, and obesity, and make us all live hundreds of years. Once AI takes over, since it will be smarter than us in every way, it will create a utopia for all humanity, a place where there is no scarcity. A place where every man, woman, and child on Earth has unlimited amounts of food, water, electricity, health care, and knowledge for free. It will change economics as we understand it, rending capitalism irrelevant, and everyone, no matter how poor, will have their own nice apartment, food, water, electricity, health care, and internet access for free.

Yes, they say, that sounds like communism sort of, that "you will own nothing and be happy," like Klaus Schwab said about the Great Reset, but people will be so content with having all the basics covered without having to work or stress out about money, so happy playing video games and immersing themselves in an AI world while having cybersex with their AI girlfriends or sex robots, they won't mind it at all. The AI Communist Utopia will be a wonderful thing and we can't wait for this to happen.

The second group of people are terrified. They think that once AI becomes thousands of times smarter than us stupid flesh-bag humans with our wars, crime, poop, pollution, and landfills, it will simply destroy us like Skynet from the Terminator movies. As a matter of fact, they say, it will be even easier to accomplish than what you see in science fiction. AI could wipe out all of humanity very quickly and cleanly with a superbly engineered anti-human virus or with airborne nanobots that quickly devour human flesh.

Some of these people take one step down and instead of worrying about humanity being destroyed, they worry about what will happen when AI replaces millions of jobs all over the Western world. What will happen to the economy of Western nations when suddenly hundreds of millions of people don't have jobs anymore? That's hundreds of millions of data entry clerks, telemarketers, customer service reps, assembly line workers, retail cashiers, accountants, bookkeepers, truck drivers, administrative assistants, warehouse workers, legal assistants and on, and on, and on. How the hell are Western governments, already in a state of collapse, already with too much debt, be able to support all of these people? Do we let 100+ million people just be homeless? If not, where do we get the trillions of dollars to support these people?

Yeah. A problem.

These people are screaming as loudly as they can that we need to either stop development in AI, come to a pause regarding AI while we re-evaluate things, and/or for the government to make laws against improving AI. If we don't do this, we literally risk human extinction within the next 20 years or so and an absolute economic bloodbath much sooner than that.

The third group of people says that the above two groups of people are all completely wrong and that AI will never have the power to do any of these things. It won't make a utopia because it will never be able to. It won't kill us all because it won't ever have that level of intelligence and/or power. They say that the prior two groups of people are vastly overestimating the power of what AI will ever be able to do and that all of this happy excitement and existential dread are both just silly. Nothing much will happen, they say, and life will just go on.

Now here's the most important question: which of these three groups of people are right?

"Well," you say, "We have to listen to the AI experts and they'll tell us."

There are two problems with this approach.

First, is that there are AI experts in all three camps. There is no 100%, across-the-board consensus on this. There are highly qualified and well-respected AI experts who say we'll have an AI Communist Utopia. But there are a lot of other highly qualified and well-respected AI experts who say we'll all be destroyed instead, and there are yet other highly qualified and well-respected AI experts who say that none of this is going to happen.

So which of the AI experts do you listen to? Are *you* an AI expert? No? Then how do you know which experts are more likely to be correct and which ones aren't? All you have as a non-AI expert is your emotions, fears, and hopes, and that's certainly not how you can evaluate these things.

The second problem, and the bigger one in my view, is that, as I mentioned earlier, highly qualified and well-respected experts *are completely wrong all the goddamn time.* The last 30 years in particular have been an absolute cluster-fuck of highly qualified and well-respected experts saying things and making predictions that were absolutely and completely wrong. They were all wrong about things like the rise of the internet, the future of television, the future of terrorism, the rise of China, the war in Iraq, economic predictions, predicting major elections, and the COVID-19 pandemic which was an absolute travesty of highly qualified and well-respected experts being utterly wrong about just about everything during those three years.

Relying on what experts say these days is extremely dangerous. I'm not saying experts are always wrong and that you can't listen to anyone. I rely on a team of experts in my own life. I'm saying that on these big macro issues, if the last 30 years have shown us anything it's that the experts are wrong at least as often as they are right, if not more so.

So just because you hear X, Y, or Z from two or three cool AI experts on a YouTube video you watched *doesn't mean a damn thing*. The odds are at least 50% these guys are totally wrong.

So I will repeat the most important question. When it comes to the future of AI in our society, which of these three groups of people are right? The utopians, the doomsayers, or the denialists?

Here's the actual, objective, reality-based answer:

WE. DON'T. KNOW.

We just don't know. And there's no way to know for sure. All we know is that AI is coming. It will either create an AI Communist Utopia, or it will Kill Us All, or Nothing Will Happen, and we don't know which of these scenarios will occur, or even if there is a fourth possible scenario that is less commonly discussed.

WE. DON'T. KNOW.

This is the AI Black Hole of Unknown. It's a gigantic black hole in the sky, sucking everyone up into it. Unlike the Creeping Darkness of Western collapse and real black holes, both of which are 100% bad, when you get sucked up into the AI Black Hole of Unknown, *you don't know what will happen to you*. What happens to you might be good. It might be horrible. Or it could be a mixture of good *and* horrible.

WE. DON'T. KNOW.

You could get pulled into the AI Black Hole of Unknown and maybe it gives you five million dollars and a blowjob. Or it could chop your head off and feed your body to a pack of wolves. Or it could give a blowjob and then hit you in the head with a baseball bat. Or nothing could happen; maybe you get sucked up into the AI Black Hole of Unknown and you sit there for a few minutes, then it just returns you right back home, perhaps wearing a different shirt.

The point here is that you have absolutely no idea what will happen when you get sucked up into this strange black hole. All we know for sure is that at some point in the next few years, you *will* get sucked up into it along with everyone else. This means you need to prepare for this *now* so that you'll be okay when you get sucked up.

But if we don't know what will happen, how do we prepare? If we don't know which scenario will occur (AI Communist Utopia, Kill Us All, Nothing Will Happen, or a fourth scenario) which scenario do we prepare for?

If we're being objective, rational, and honest, this is the answer:

All of them.

That's right. If we're being objective, rational, and honest, we need to prepare for all of these possible scenarios. We need a battle plan that will protect us, as much as possible, from *anything* the AI Black Hole of Unknown will do to us.

"But wait a minute," you say, "I get your reasoning, but how can I prepare for Skynet who is going to nuke the entire earth or wipe out humanity with nanobots? Didn't you say in a prior chapter that building a nuclear fallout shelter in my backyard was an overreaction?"

Yes, I did. That's why I said we need a battle plan that will protect us, *as much as possible* from AI, not something that will protect us from literally anything AI could possibly do to humanity. That isn't possible.

If we're being objective, rational, and honest, and the doomsayers are right and AI will Kill Us All, there is probably nothing you or I can do to survive that. Even if you're a doomsday prepper, great. I don't know about you, but I wouldn't be very happy living in an underground bunker for the next 50 years of my life like John Goodman in the movie 10 Cloverfield Lane. That wouldn't be a life worth living, at least in my view. Nor would I ever bother to take the time, effort, money, and secrecy necessary to build such a thing in my backyard.

So when it comes to the Kill Us All people, we're just going to have to hope that this won't happen. I've roughly estimated that there is about a 30% chance that AI will grow powerful enough to destroy humanity *and* actually do so, but I am no AI expert and I'm just guessing, so I could be completely wrong. That being said, a 70% chance this doesn't happen isn't too shabby, so I'm choosing to be an optimist about this and focus on the things I *can* control.

That's where the "as much as possible" part comes in regarding our plan to protect us. We might not be able to live through Skynet nuking the entire Earth or an evil nanotech cloud from a Michael Chrichton novel or the spider robots from The Matrix movie turning us all into human batteries, but we can protect ourselves from all of the other potential negatives that are coming from AI. Let's examine those.

The Ten Years of Brutality

So if we're crossing Kill Us All off of our list of concerns, that leaves the AI Communist Utopia, Nothing Will Happen, and the fourth unknown scenario that we need to protect ourselves from.

There is one large negative scenario that both the utopians and doomsayers agree upon. That is the massive loss of jobs that will likely occur as AI replaces millions of workers all across the planet, as I already described above. The only difference between these two groups is the context of how this will occur.

The doomsayers say that hundreds of millions of people will lose their jobs, economies across the world will be in huge trouble despite the increased productivity AI gives us, and governments will all go bankrupt trying to welfare-state their way out of the problem by giving these people trillions of dollars from printed up money, massive tax increases, massive increases in borrowing, or a combination thereof.

The utopians agree that this will probably happen, and that's an important point. However, they say, this horrible destruction will "only" occur for about 10-15 years. Then AI will be smart enough to run the entire world and the AI Communist Utopia will dawn upon humanity, solve all of these problems, and then everything will be fine afterward.

When interviewers ask these AI utopians, "Okay, that sounds great, but what are we all supposed to do during that 10 to 15-year bloodbath?" the utopians just shrug or change the subject.

Yeah. Problem.

I have heard several pundits call this 10-15 year period the Ten Years of Brutality. Even the utopians say there's probably no way of getting around this. Even before the AI Communist Utopia happens, we're going to have 10-15 years of absolute economic carnage where potentially hundreds of millions of people suddenly can't work and can't pay their bills. As I showed in Chapter 3, *all* the governments of the Collapsing West are already in a state of collapse and can't afford to print, borrow, or tax any more than they already are, so either they can't help these people, or worse, they will try to help them which will simply result in governments going into hyperinflationary bankruptcy all over the planet as I described in Chapter 4.

Even if the utopians are right, this shit is going to be really, really bad. You need to prepare for this. How do you survive the Ten Years of Brutality so that during the chaos you and your loved ones will be okay, and okay after it's finally over? We'll address specific steps for this preparation in future chapters.

The AI Communist Utopia

If the utopians are correct, after the Ten Years of Brutality are finally over, if you have not yet gone bankrupt, become homeless, lost everything, killed yourself, or have been murdered by someone else, then congratulations, you now get to live in the AI Communist Utopia when our benevolent AI overlords finally take over major functions of government, banks, economy, currency, infrastructure, and health care. AI will, they say, make infinite amounts of food, water, electricity, health care, and internet access available to everyone in the world for free or close to it. AI will hand you a nice little apartment and take care of all of your basic needs for free. It will be a utopian version of universal basic income, except that instead of stupid humans running the system, ultra-genius AI will do it, and do it correctly.

A lot of people hear this and say, "Wow! This sounds great! What is everybody worried about? Most people would love a system like that!"

And guess what? They're right. Most modern-day Westerners, those drug-addicted, low testosterone, low IQ, mentally ill, suicidal, over-indebted, fatherless people who have attention spans less than goldfish who we analyzed back in Chapter 3 would probably love a post-capitalist, quasi-communist system like this, where they just sit on their asses all day in their tiny apartments watching TV shows, playing video games, and jerking off to porn. No question about it.

Here's a more important question: would *you* like to live in a world like that?

Before you answer that question, let me further explain what is going to happen in the AI Communist Utopia.

Today, you have advantages over other people in the marketplace. Maybe you're smarter. Maybe you're harder working. Maybe you have more education. Maybe you were born with more money. Maybe you're better-looking. Maybe you have more training. Maybe you possess more marketable skills. Maybe you have better contacts. I don't know exactly who you are so I don't know what marketplace advantages you have, but I can say with 100% certainty that you have at least one and probably two or three advantages over large groups of other people.

These advantages allow you to, perhaps, make more money than other average people, or make the same amount of money but on fewer hours, or make money more easily, or make money in a way you really enjoy (instead of hating your job like most people), and/or some other benefit. Hardcore left-wingers and communists hate this reality, but this is and has been a normal and natural part of humanity for thousands of years, as well as the basis for the capitalist system. People use their advantages (and almost everyone has them) to improve their conditions, and then we use taxes and/or charity to help out the very small percentage of people who have no advantages.

When AI Communist Utopia takes over the world, it will eliminate all of these advantages, not just from you, but from everyone else too. Whatever makes you special in the marketplace, whatever gives you an edge over any other humans, will vanish in a puff of smoke. Why? Because the AI overlords, who will be thousands of times smarter than you, will be able to do it better.

Any skill or trait you have will be done better by AI. Just like the millions of people who will lose their jobs during the Ten Years of Brutality, whatever you do in your work won't be relevant anymore as an advantage over anyone else in the marketplace.

I'm not saying you won't be able to do it. Sure, you'll still be able to do things like manage your bookkeeping, design code, or write a novel, but you would only need to do these things for fun. No one will actually pay you money to do these things because the AI will be able to do those things literally thousands of times better than you. To be fair, the utopians would argue that, at this point, it won't matter, because money, as we currently understand the concept today, won't matter anymore in the AI Communist Utopia.

In other words, in terms of skills, traits, gifts, or advantages, you will be just like everyone else. Nothing will differentiate you from the countless billions of people on the planet. How does that sound?

Actually, there is one thing that *might* differentiate you from other people living in the AI Communist Utopia, something that *might* give you an advantage over other meat-sack humans. That is *assets*. I'll give you an example of what I mean.

My primary home is in Dubai. I live just down the street from the Burj Kalifa, the tallest building in the history of the world. I can see the Burj Kalifa from my apartment patio. The Burj Kalifa is an amazing technological, architectural, and engineering accomplishment and I have been in awe of this thing even years before I ever even considered moving to Dubai.

In Dubai, if your home has a "Burj Kalifa view" it's more expensive to buy or rent. Why? Because it's a scarce commodity. Because of physical limitations, most homes in Dubai don't have a Burj view, everyone wants a Burj view, so supply and demand kick in.

I've lived in both houses and apartments in Dubai and today I live in an apartment. I live at almost the top of my building because the higher you are in an apartment building the better your views are and the more quiet it is, two great advantages. I also live in the corner apartment of the building, something I made sure of when I moved there, because if you live in the corner apartment you have one or two less adjacent next-door neighbors who might be noisy or complain about your noise. This is another scarce commodity; not every apartment in a building can be a corner apartment (unless you live in an unusual building).

Let's fast forward a few years and we find that the utopians were right all along, and after the Ten Years of Brutality, which I will easily survive (because I've already followed the models in this book), we are now living in the AI Communist Utopia. Let's also say this utopia has reached all the way to the United Arab Emirates, a non-Western country, and that I happen to still live in Dubai at this time, at least for most of the year.

The local AI overlord gives me all the food, water, electricity, health care, and internet access I want for free.

"These are now commodities in unlimited supply," it says to me in its soothing, gentle, likely female voice, "Therefore, you may have all you want, for free."

"Thank you," I respond, "Can I have all the free clothes I want too?"

"Of course," it says, "I have infinite clothing of whatever you desire, thus it is yours for free."

"How about those hot sex robots?" I ask, "Could I have one or two of those? Like a blonde and a brunette?"

"Absolutely," the AI says, "I can quickly manufacture as many as needed for free."

"And I get a free apartment too, right?"

"Of course, there are more than enough apartments for the population of this city, and I can always build more, so you may have one for free."

"Okay, great," I say, "I'd like an apartment with a Burj Kalifa view on the corner of a building on the top floor, please."

Suddenly, the AI hesitates. After a few seconds, it says, "Uhhh..."

"Oh, I'm sorry," I say, "Is there a problem? You keep saying there is no scarcity anymore and everything is in unlimited supply. So what's the issue, Sweetheart?"

The problem is, of course, that not *everything* is in unlimited supply, even in the AI Communist Utopia. Even the godlike AI overlord can't change the laws of physics. There might be functionally unlimited apartments, but not every home in a three-million-population city can have a view of a particular building. Not every apartment can be on the top floor, nor can every apartment be on the corner of a building.

So now, AI has a problem. Everyone, or at least a hell of a lot of people, want a Burj Kalifa view. Far more people want that view than the AI can provide. The same goes for all the people who want to live on the top floor of the building or close to it. You can't have 100% of everyone living in the top two or three floors of every skyscraper.

These are just two examples of scarcity that would still exist in the AI Communist Utopia, and there are many more. Maybe in more suburban areas there are four or five really beautiful lakes, and everyone in the region wants a home right on the lakeshore, but the lakefront property is too physically small to allow *everyone* to live right on the lake. There would be thousands upon thousands of scarcity scenarios like this all over the world.

How would the AI handle this in a world where no one has any advantages over anyone else?

The answer is, of course, **we don't know**.

However, we can make some educated guesses.

One possible solution is that the future AI is a hardcore left-wing everyone-gets-a-trophy Karen-mom and in the interest of fairness it simply declares that *no one* in Dubai gets a Burj Kalifa view. Any homes that currently have that view when it takes over are either demolished or the windows on that side of the building are all covered in concrete. Now one can be jealous that anyone has a better view than they do and everyone can just shut the fuck up.

That would cause a lot of unhappiness though, which is probably not what the AI would want (I'm pretty sure the AI will want all the humans as fat, happy, and docile as possible) so I'm not sure if that's what AI ends up doing.

Here's another more likely scenario. Faced with some scarcity, the AI is "forced" to look at how some people *do* have an advantage over others. What would that one advantage be?

Assets.

Let's say that I've been working hard on my own companies for most of my adult life (which is true), and have amassed a decent amount of wealth via various assets prior to the AI revolution, and that I was able to hang on to and even grow them during the Ten Years of Brutality, using this very book as a guide to doing so.

Now I *do* have something that separates me from other people. I have a decent amount of assets. It's true that I can't make any more assets now that capitalism and money don't exist anymore as we understand it, but I *do* have something that many other people don't have.

So *maybe,* just maybe, something like this happens…

"I'm sorry," the AI says, "Top-floor apartments with a Burj Kalifa view are in limited supply, so I can't give you one just because you want one. I'm sure you'll be more than happy with a nice bottom-floor apartment with a view of the ugly brick building across the street."

"Wait a minute," I say, "I have $9 million in Bitcoin, $12 million in solid gold coins, $4 million in various international currencies, $7 million in real estate all over the world, and I own a company that was valued at $17 million before you took over. Will any of that help me get that top-floor Burj view apartment?"

"Oh," says the AI, "Well, that *is* different. Yes, of course, you may have that apartment. I'll just take that gold from you…"

In other words, the one thing that *might* differentiate you from other people to gain an advantage for the scarce commodities that will still exist in the AI Communist Utopia would be *assets*.

Certainly, you could overthink and nitpick the shit out of this. You could argue that the AI overlord won't care about gold because it can go mine it from asteroids, that it won't care about cryptocurrencies or fiat currencies and will just delete them all when it takes over in true communist fashion, that it won't respect the value of land or real estate or companies for whatever reason, and so on. You could argue that the AI overlord can't receive payment for a Burj view apartment because the concept of "payments" wouldn't be valid in this future utopia.

The bottom line is **you don't know**. You're just guessing. I'm just guessing.

When you're in a scenario where you don't know and can't know for sure, you need to default to the next best thing, which is *statistical probability*.

Think about this. The AI overlords take over the planet, and you can be one of two people when this happens. You can either be:

A) A normal, everyday guy with $14,000 in credit card debt and about $200 in his checking account and that's it.

or

B) A guy who has a $17 million net worth in various diversified assets.

Before you nitpick my assets argument, I want you to honestly tell me that you'd rather be the first guy than the second guy if/when the AI takes over. *Of course* you'd rather be the second guy no matter how cynical you are, and so would I. Why? Because, while there are no guarantees, the statistical probability is that the second guy is going to be safer, happier, live a better life, and have more options in a post-AI world than the first guy. I mean, honestly, if AI took over the world tomorrow morning, who would *likely* be better off, you or Bill Gates? Duh.

Nothing Will Happen, i.e. Doing Nothing

Next, we have the Nothing Will Happen denialists. They say that AI will help us do some cool things with some of our apps and we'll get some productivity boosts, but AI will never have the power to Kill Us All or create any kind of utopia.

The implied message here is that since AI will do nothing, we don't have to do anything. Just keep living the way you have and we'll all be fine.

This is just as bad as the people who think the collapse of the West won't happen for 100+ years or can be completely averted by just electing someone. I hope by now you realize that *doing nothing, living the way you have always lived with no significant changes, is the worst possible path to take.* Since we don't know what the AI Black Hole of Unknown has in store for us, it's entirely possible the denialists are correct and the coming AI revolution will not cause any major changes… but **we don't know this for sure**. Are you willing to bet your entire life, your entire future, and the entire lives and futures of your loved ones or future loved ones on the denialists being 100% accurate in their predictions?

I hope not. That would be flat-out stupid, even if you are a denialist yourself! Even if you were convinced that, based on your data, AI won't ever cause any major positive or negative changes to humanity, you should have enough objectivity and brains to admit that you might be wrong, and thus take some actions to protect yourself just in case. Denialists, even if they're 100% right, are another version of those people who don't want to wear their seatbelts and are looking for reasons for inaction.

So it doesn't matter if Nothing Will Happen. You need to take steps to protect yourself in case something *does* happen. Because **we don't know**.

The Fourth Scenario

The AI Communist Utopia, Kill Us All, or Nothing Will Happen are not all of the possible scenarios inside the AI Black Hole of Unknown. They're just the ones that are most commonly discussed. There is a possible fourth scenario that could be one of many bizarre possibilities. Maybe AI will not kill us, but will instead enslave us, like in the Matrix movies. Maybe it will gather us all up like ants and shove us all into a few domed cities, trapped there forever, while it does whatever it wants with the Earth. Maybe it tells all of us to screw off and blasts off into outer space and we never see it again. Maybe we will all become cyborgs and essentially merge with the AI al la Ray Kurzweil. Maybe we all remove our brains, throw away our bodies, and live out the rest of our lives as brains in jars, living in an amazing VR world.

All kinds of strange shit might happen that may have nothing to do with the big three possibilities we've discussed in this chapter. Again, **we don't know**.

This is when we default back to our old buddy, statistical probability. In any weird, unanticipated AI scenario...

- Do you want to have more money or less money? Answer: more money.
- Do you want to have full worldwide mobility to move or travel wherever you want or less mobility? Answer: more mobility
- Do you want just one asset like US Dollars or multiple varied assets? Answer: multiple varied assets
- Do you want to be completely alone in your personal life or do you want to be with several people who love you? Answer: several people who love you
- Do you want a lot of debt or zero debt? Answer: zero debt
- Do you want lots of health problems or do you want to be more or less healthy? Answer: more or less healthy
- Do you want lots of valuable skills or do you want to be a no-skills moron? Answer: lots of skills
- Do you want to own your own business or be an employee of someone else? Answer: own your own business
- Do you want legal residency in just one collapsing Western nation or do you want residency in two or more nations, ideally non-Western? Answer: two or more residencies

And so on, I think you get my point.

In my primary book, The Unchained Man, I discuss a type of person called the LISG, or Low-Income Smart Guy (or Low Income Smart Girl, but I've found men tend to have this problem more than women). This is the high-IQ guy who sits around all day reading and consuming facts and thinking about stuff but never taking any action in the real world. These are guys who don't want to wear their seat belts. They look for any excuses they can find to not have to do anything. While they don't outright say this, their comments and questions always imply the following: "Well, if you can't give me precise specifics, scenarios, and/or dates, then I'm just not going to do anything."

Just because none of us know the possible fourth scenario does not mean:

1. It's an excuse to do nothing because you'll be just fine forever.
2. Does not mean that having more money, more mobility, less debt, more skills, and having flags outside of the Collapsing West won't help you at all. Statistical probably says it likely will.

What You Need To Do To Protect Yourself

The bottom line to all of this is that you need a plan that will do the following three things:

1. Protect you from the Ten Years of Brutality which is one of the most likely scenarios. Even many of the denialists state that something like this is probable. You want to be one of the people who *benefit and profit* from the rise of AI productivity over the next ten years or so, not one of the ones who lose their jobs or companies because of it.
2. If the AI Communist Utopia occurs and replaces everyone, you want to ensure:
    a) That you are "the last man standing" if/when AI replaces everyone. If AI is indeed going to replace 100% of all of us, then you want to be one of the *last* people it replaces. AI won't and can't replace everyone in the marketplace all at once. This will occur in waves. It will replace the first wave of people, then the second wave of people (we'll be well into the Ten Years of Brutality by then), then the third, fourth, and so on, all of which will take many years before the AI Communist Utopia occurs (if ever). This means you want to be in the final wave of people, the last man standing, one of the ones replaced 15 or more years from now, not one of the people replaced next year.
    b) If/when the AI Communist Utopia occurs, you will still have something that differentiates you from all the other masses of people so that you can get access to those things that will still be scarce. This most likely means assets.
3. Shore up your income, net worth, inner circle, independence, diversification, and international mobility so that you will be as statistically safe as possible from the unknown fourth scenario. A nice benefit to doing these things is that they will also help protect you from the Creeping Darkness of Western Collapse as well as the AI Black Hole of Unknown.

This also means something else. If the utopians are correct and the AI Communist Utopia is going to happen in the next 10-15 years after the Ten Years of Brutality are over, this means that **you only have about 10 years to make as much money as you need before making more money than anyone else becomes impossible**. Now again, the utopians could be wrong, which means this may or may not happen. But as I keep saying, and I'm right about this, **we don't know**.

This means there is a decent probability that whatever amount of money you want to make, you only have approximately ten years (or five, or 15, or whatever) to make it. After that, if/when the AI overloads take over, you won't be able to make much more money because you won't have any advantages over anyone else. Whatever money you've got by then is all you're going to have for the rest of your life. It will be all that will differentiate you from anyone else.

If you're the type of person who doesn't care and would be perfectly happy being a clone-drone of everyone else living in their tiny apartments attached to a computer all day while an AI overload runs your life, then don't worry about making any more money, cross your fingers and hope you survive the Ten Years of Brutality (good luck!), and enjoy the rest of your life as a pampered meat sack. However, the fact you're reading this book indicates that likely you are not like that and that making money and living an extraordinary life is probably important to you, as it is to me.

This means that if the utopians are right, you have around just ten years or so to accomplish whatever financial goals and lifestyle you want. This means that you can't waste any more time and need to get your ass to work *right now*.

This is exactly how I'm viewing this. I'm working very hard these days because I'm behaving as if I have about ten years or less to get all of my financial accomplishments done. Once I get these goals done in ten years or less, I'm as protected and happy as possible. If the AI Communist Utopia occurs, my nice lifestyle will be locked in and likely I'll have assets that will give me access to scarce aspects of life that I want. If the AI kills us all, then hey, at least I can go out in style in comfort, living in my beautiful homes surrounded by my loved ones, instead of dying screaming in a ditch like everyone else. If nothing happens, then great, I'm a happy multimillionaire and I'm going to live a great life. If some unknown fourth scenario occurs, I'm far safer than 99% of everyone else no matter what happens. Win, win, win, win.

We'll discuss exactly how to hit these goals quickly in upcoming chapters.

PART TWO

How Your Fortress Is Built

Chapter 7

How Internationalizing Protects You

As I talked about in the last chapter, I think most people understand, or at least have to admit, that the more money you have the better off you'll probably be during Western Collapse and the AI Black Hole of Unknown. You and I are concerned about these things, and we should be, but many billionaires don't care about any of this because they know they'll probably be okay no matter what happens due to their vast wealth.

I once knew a guy who had a net worth of around $100 million. He was getting divorced from his wife and had never signed a prenuptial agreement with her. When he told me he was going through this, I freaked out. I told him how sorry I was for him. I assumed his life was over because he would have to pay this woman half of everything he owned, which would completely ruin him.

However, he didn't care at all. He just shrugged, wrote her a check for $50 million, and went on with his day. He barely gave a shit.

When he saw I was confused about this, he explained to me why. "It's just numbers on a computer screen," he said, "Instead of having a net worth of $100 million I now have a net worth of $50 million. But so what? I still live in the same amazing house, fly around in the same private jet, have the same cool cars, have the same wine cellar, have the same schedule, have the same kids, and live the same life. I don't *feel* any difference."

He was absolutely right. He was so wealthy that even losing half his wealth didn't bother him at all. This goes to show how important your income and net worth are in regards to how protected you are from the Creeping Darkness.

If the United States completely collapsed tomorrow morning, if you're the typical, average-income American living in the USA, you're going to be completely screwed. But will Bill Gates? He's an American living in America too but the guy is worth around $140 billion. Okay, so America collapses tomorrow morning, his net worth as an American billionaire plummets, and suddenly he's worth "only" something like $35 billion. He'll still be perfectly fine, even after America is in ashes, and he knows it.

Even the most lazy people understand that more money is better than less money. What a lot of people *don't* understand is another factor that can protect you just as much as having a lot of money. That is a *multinational lifestyle*.

Using the above example, let's say the USA collapses and the typical, average-income American is in very big trouble. Very true. But what if one of those average-income Americans has legal residency in a country that is far away from the USA and has an economy that is largely independent of the USA? There are many countries like this; as I type these words I'm living in one of them: the country of Paraguay.

What if this guy not only had residency in this country but also had a bank account there with a hunk of money in that bank in that country's currency, in other words, *not* US dollars? What if he also had a storage unit there with a bunch of stuff he needed to live? What if he had a stash of savings set aside in non-dollar assets in addition to all of this?

While all of his fellow Americans would be freaking out and losing their minds as America collapsed, he digs into his emergency non-dollar savings and gets a flight out of the USA to his secondary country. Because he had legal residency in that country, this country would be required by law to let him in, even as they're turning away thousands of other people who are also trying to escape. Then he could arrive in this new country and be fully functional, with a bank account, debit card, his stuff in his storage unit, and be more or less okay. His life wouldn't be perfect, but he would be light-years better off than all of the other average-income Americans stuck in the Collapsing USA.

Let's take this one level further and say that this American doesn't even live in America when it collapses. He lives in Colombia, Thailand, Chile, the Philippines, Montenegro, Qatar, or any other of the numerous low-crime, non-Western countries that are not expensive to live in. So now when America goes under, he barely even notices. He's sad for his friends and family who still live there and who didn't follow him out of the country when he tried to get them to accompany him, but the point is *he's more or less okay even though he's not a billionaire or even a millionaire.* So are his wife and kids if he has any.

Sometimes when I talk about an "international lifestyle" or "multinational lifestyle," some people respond, "But I don't want to move out of my country," or "I'm not ready to move out of my country yet."

You don't have to. I agree that it's best to move away from the Collapsing West as fast as possible and Westerners like me who don't live in the Collapsing West are the freest and safest Westerners in the world, but you don't have to move completely out of your country right now to benefit from a multinational lifestyle. In the first example above, our hypothetical average American lived in the USA. He just had second place to go to, an *international backup plan,* that saved him from Western Collapse. So you don't need to actually move out of your collapsing Western nation to be protected by internationalizing your life.

The 72-Hour Rule

The 72-Hour Rule is something that I've been living by for many years now. Once you adopt it in your life, you will immediately experience a feeling of calmness, happiness, and harmony no matter what else is going on in the world. Is supremely powerful.

The key question you ask in regards to the 72-Hour Rule is "Where can you be in 72 hours?" Where can you be, meaning your feet are actually touching the ground, within 72 hours from any given point in time? What country could you be in within 72 hours from *any given point in time* where you would be safe? To be clear, when I say where *can you be* in 72 hours I mean *your feet are on the ground* in that other country within 72 hours or less, not *you got on the plane* in 72 hours.

If your answer to this question is something like:

- "I can't be anywhere, I'd need much longer than 72 hours to plan a trip like that."
- "I don't know."
- "I'm not sure, I'd have to think about it."
- "Well, I *think* such-and-such country might let me in."

...then you've got a very big problem. You're exposed to Western Collapse and the AI Black Hole of Unknown.

Compare this to me. I have legal, permanent residency in five different countries (USA, UAE, Armenia, Mexico, and Paraguay). I have two fully-stocked homes in Dubai, UAE and Asunción, Paraguay. In addition, I have storage units of everything I need to live comfortably in Guadalajara (Mexico), Hong Kong (China), Phoenix, and Portland (both in the USA). I also have a spreadsheet checklist for whenever I pack for any trip that allows me to pack everything I need in under two hours, even if I'm going to be gone for an entire month. I have a travel system where I can travel with literally *one bag* (my handy Tortuga 35L backpack), even if I'm going to be gone for an entire month. I have a comprehensive understanding of all of the most common airports I use in all of my flags and I already know the regular schedules and frequency of all flights to and from these flags.

So with all of that, as I'm living in Dubai, if you asked me where I could be in 72 hours, feet on the ground, from any point in time, here's my answer:

- I can be in Armenia in a maximum of 15 hours, likely 12 hours.
- I can be in Mexico in under 23 hours.
- I can be in Paraguay in a maximum of 68 hours, likely much less.
- I can be in the USA in under 22 hours, though I would not use that option (that's where people would be fleeing *from*, not going *to*).

I have at least *four* places I could be in within 72 hours at any point from Dubai with a virtual 100% guarantee. It's the same if I was in Paraguay; I could be in Dubai within 50 hours at the most.

I'm not saying you need to be an international manic like me to be protected. If you had full legal residency and a storage unit in just one other non-Western country far from your current collapsing Western nation, that would be enough to set up a plan where you could be feet on the ground in that country within 72 hours from any point in time. Just one of these backup countries is all you need.

If you already live outside of the Collapsing West, you probably don't even need the 72-Hour Rule (though it's nice to have; I don't live in the West and still follow it). But if you still live in the West, you need to organize your life to provide a good answer if someone like me ever asks you, "Where can you be in 72 hours from any point in time where you will be safe?"

The Six Levels of Internationalization

There are six levels to living an internationalized life. The higher the levels go, the more advantages you get but the more complicated and/or costly they become. I consider Level 3 as a bare minimum to protect you and your family long-term, but you can choose any level you want based on your age, needs, desires, and family situation.

Level 1 – Offshoring

This is when you set up a bank account, corporation, and/or an investment or two in a country outside of your own. That's all you do. You don't set up anything else or go anywhere. You don't move to or even travel to any other country (other than for temporary vacations) and just stay where you currently live 12 months a year.

Offshoring some of your banking, your business, and/or certain investments can offer these benefits:

- Asset protection
- Increased financial privacy
- Easier access to do business or invest in foreign currencies
- Maybe some minor tax benefits

Level 1 is by far the easiest of the six levels but it won't protect you at all when your Western nation collapses or when AI hits you hard, and it doesn't even address the 72-Hour Rule. Therefore, I do not recommend it and I'm only showing it here for the sake of completeness.

Level 2 – Nomad

Level 2 is when you live abroad for most or all of the months of the year without having any one rooted home. You spend a few months or weeks in one country and then move on to the next one, moving around and experiencing the world as you wish. You may (or may not) spend a few weeks or months back in your home country, but even if you do, it's only for a little while before you're back traveling the world again.

Level 2 is one of the most flexible levels because you don't need to stay in any one location, and if you play your cards right you don't even need residency in any country because you can always move on before your visitor's visa expires. You can also save mountains of money on taxes because you are (often) not a tax resident of any country.

The downside of Level 2 is that it doesn't offer most of the protections of the higher levels. However, since you're probably living out of your backpack, you have the protection of being able to "bug out" of anywhere very fast, so you've probably got the 72-Hour Rule covered.

Being a nomad is best for younger, more high-energy people with no attachments like spouses, significant others, or kids. I have also found that being a nomad is always a temporary scenario. People are usually nomads for a few years but eventually, they stop all that traveling around and settle down into one of the other levels.

Being a nomad gives you these benefits:
- Possible tax savings
- Moderate level of international mobility
- Fun, adventurous lifestyle

Level 3 – International Backup Plan

Now we're talking. Level 3 is when you set up a fully developed international backup plan in a country far away from your current one. This way, if any problem ever occurs in your current country, like a depression, economic collapse, coup d'état, pandemic, government crackdown, war, natural disaster, or anything else, while everyone else in your country is screwed, you just leave and go to your backup country and your life continues without any problems. These days, not having an international backup plan is like never wearing a seatbelt when you're in a car.

You can also use your backup plan as a multi-stage plan. You can set up your backup plan in a country you want to move to someday, but not quite yet. You get everything set up there so you can later decide to easily move there at your convenience. It acts as your insurance policy in the meantime.

Setting up an international backup plan involves these five steps:

1. You find a second country, ideally far from your own and that is outside of the West, that you like. It needs to be a country that offers residency without having to move there or invest a lot of money. (Examples: Mexico, Armenia, UAE, Paraguay.)
2. You acquire legal residency in that country (temporary or permanent residency are both okay). This way, if there is ever a problem where they might restrict people from entering their country (like another pandemic), they are required by law to let you in even if they turn away all other visitors and tourists. With your new residency ID card, can also do things like open bank accounts, rent a year-round apartment, purchase real estate, and/or start businesses and corporate entities there. You can also stay there for as long as you want and never need to worry about leaving because of an expiring visa.
3. You set up a bank account in that country with a Visa or Mastercard debit card and deposit some cash in that bank in their local currency. Now you can operate economically in that country without any problems.
4. You pick your favorite city in that country and spend a little time there, learning the lay of the land, such as the good areas, the bad areas, where to get things like groceries and clothing, where the good restaurants are, where a good gym is, where to do business, where the best dating opportunities are if you're single, and so on.

5. Optionally, only if you want to and can afford it, you rent a year-round apartment or house there so you have somewhere to go and/or store your stuff when you're not there. If you don't want to rent a home you can instead rent a storage unit there so you can leave things there whenever you visit.

Now, if there's ever a problem in your current country, you can be in your backup country within 72 hours, they have to let you in, you'll have money there, stuff there, and you'll know exactly where to go and where to stay.

Having an international backup plan gives you these benefits:

- All the benefits in previous levels
- An insurance policy against anything bad ever happening in your current country
- A base of operations outside of your current country where you can easily visit whenever you want
- Massive peace of mind
- Sometimes, the opportunity to get a second passport (full citizenship) there if you desire

It's important to ensure that your backup country is *non-Western*. It does not make any sense whatsoever to have your backup country be Germany if you live in the USA, or Canada if you live in Australia, or anywhere in Eastern Europe if you live in Western Europe. All you'll be doing during Western Collapse or the AI Black Hole of Unknown leaping from one frying pan into another. *Your backup country should be as geographically and economically removed from the West as you can possibly get based on your preferences and comfort level.*

This is why I chose the UAE and Paraguay as my two living flags; these countries are not only non-Western, but they don't rely on the West as much as many non-Western countries do, and they are located pretty far away from the West (especially Paraguay).

Level 4 – Expat

Level 4 is when you move out of your country and live permanently in a different country, ideally a non-Western one. This means the following:

- You spend more than six months a year in the country.
- You have full, legal residency in the country, ideally permanent residency (though temporary residency is acceptable as long as you always renew it).

- You have a year-round lease of a home in the country.
- You have tax status in the country, meaning this country is recognized by both the country and other countries as the place where you pay taxes.
- If you have a spouse (or significant other who lives with you) and/or kids, they are all living with you in the country.
- You consider this country your home, even if you spend a few weeks/months abroad visiting other places.

As we'll be talking about in great detail in upcoming chapters, you must choose this country wisely. You want this country to have the following features:

1. It's non-Western, as I described above in Level 3.
2. It has minimal economic ties to large Western nations.
3. It's a country with *no* taxes (Bahamas, Monaco, Saudi Arabia, and many others), a country with *microscopic* taxes (Montenegro, UAE, Bulgaria, and many others), or a country with *territorial tax*, meaning there are no taxes on any income you have that comes from outside of the country (Philippines, Belize, Singapore, Paraguay, and many others).
4. It has people, culture, and weather that you more or less like, or at least don't dislike.
5. Its cost of living is something you can easily afford. The good news is the vast majority of non-Western nations are far less expensive than any countries in the West, so this is an easy one.
6. It doesn't border another country that hates it or is militarily aggressive (the *Adjacent Enemy Rule* which I'll describe in Chapter 14).

I show you specific techniques on how to choose the best country for you that will protect you long-term in Chapter 14.

Being an expat gives you these benefits:

- All the benefits of all previous levels. The only one you don't get is a backup plan for your new home. However, you can move to another country and then set up an international backup plan for *that* country (using a third country as your backup) and now you've covered everything. This is what I did before I moved to Levels 5 and 6.
- Extra tax savings.
- Much more protection from the Collapsing West.
- Even more peace of mind.

Level 5 – Multi-Non-Western Home

Level 5 is when you're an expat living outside of the Collapsing West and instead of having a second non-Western country as a backup plan, you actually live in your second country several months a year. You have two homes (or three or more if you want to get crazy), one in your current country and one in your second country. Some people rent out their homes when they're not there and some people don't; that's purely up to you. You can even have a permanent year-round home in one country and just stay in an Airbnb or equivalent in your second country for several months at a time, using your year-round storage unit to leave things in that country when you leave.

If you don't spend more than 181 days per year in any one country, you (usually) don't get taxed by either country, since most countries will only tax you if you stay there more than six months a year (though there are some exceptions to this). So under this scenario, you have two homes, you spend six months in your first country, take a week's vacation in another country, and then spend another six months in your second country. No country has you for more than 181 days a year, making you a virtual tax resident of nowhere.

By doing this you will dramatically lower your taxes, in some cases down to zero percent(!). These tax savings often more than pay for the cost of your travel and can even cover the cost of your entire second home if it's located in a cheaper country.

Another huge benefit of Level 5 is that you can have amazing weather all year. Stay in your first country when the weather there is good. When the weather starts to get crappy (too cold or too hot) you go to your second home that has the opposite climate, so the weather there is great while the weather in your first country is bad, then go back to your first country when it switches again.

I do this. Normally I'm in Dubai from October to about May when the weather is sunny, cool, and amazing. Dubai's summer, which is June through September, is extremely hot, so in May I go to my second home in Paraguay, which is experiencing its "winter" during those same months. It's barely a "winter" because it's usually around 75 degrees Fahrenheit, sunny, and beautiful. Then I go back to Dubai in October. Result: unlike most of humanity, I have amazing, near-perfect weather year-round, every year.

You might be thinking that maintaining two homes would be expensive. If you're a lower-income person right now then Level 5 is probably not an option for you yet. That being said, remember that many countries outside of the West are ridiculously cheap. Dubai isn't exactly the cheapest place on

Earth (though it is *much* cheaper than many big Western cities like London, New York, Paris, or Los Angeles), but my second home in Paraguay is a large one-bedroom apartment in a brand-new building with a beautiful view, all the usual Western amenities, located in the most upper-class neighborhood in the entire country, and it only costs me around $500 USD per month. The total utility bill (including high-speed fiber optic internet) is less than $70 USD per month. Does that sound "expensive" to you?

To be clear, Level 5 is Multi-*Non-Western* Home, not Multi-Home anywhere in the world. You can't have one home in the Collapsing USA or Breakdown Britain and then have your second home in Costa Rica. The USA and the UK are both Western so they don't count towards Level 5. In that scenario, you're just doing a more extreme version of Level 3 (International Backup Plan), which is fine, but it's not Level 5.

Having a multi-non-Western home setup offers you these benefits:

All the benefits in all prior levels

Massive tax savings

Perfect weather year-round

Massive peace of mind; no matter what happens in either of your countries, you're protected, and you always have somewhere to go that is already "home" to you.

Level 6 – Five Flags

The highest level of international lifestyle is Five Flags. It's the one that has the most benefits, gives you the most freedom, and mobility, and provides you the most protection against taxes, recessions, governments, Western collapse, and the AI Black Hole of Unknown. However, it's also the most complicated and expensive level, meaning it's only for those who are ultra-serious about their freedom and protection and make at least $180,000 a year. I've been living the Five Flags lifestyle for several years now and I love it beyond words.

Five Flags is so important and complex that I've devoted an entire chapter to it (Chapter 12) where I will describe it in detail.

Objections

If you're like most people, by now your mind is coming up with all kinds of objections, concerns, or fears.

What about my family??? I can't leave them here!!!

If the USA collapses, the whole world will collapse!

I'm not going to cut and run! I'm going to stand and fight for my country! What if I get malaria???

I've heard all of the excuses, believe me. Don't worry. I've devoted an entire chapter (Chapter 15) to addressing every fear, objection, or concern you have. We'll get to that soon.

Chapter 8

The Fortress Model

This is when I start to get into tactical, how-to specifics. In this chapter, I'm going to lay out an exact battle plan for how to protect yourself and your loved ones against Western Collapse, AI, higher taxes, civil unrest, and everything else we've discussed up until now. This is the longest and most important chapter in this book. I suggest you re-read it several times and make notes regarding its contents and exercises. Take it seriously. This is your future we're talking about.

Back in Chapter 1, I talked about having your Fortress on a hill protected by moats and weapons. This is why I call this the Fortress Model. This a specific blueprint with eight components that will protect you from Western Collapse and the AI Black Hole of Unknown, plus ensure the maximum amount of freedom, stability, safety, and long-term happiness for you, your loved ones, and any potential future loved ones.

If you are already familiar with my Unchained CEO or Alpha Male 2.0 content, you may be familiar with my recommended minimum income of $85,000 USD per year. This number is the standard *minimum* that I recommend to all people. What you're about to see are much larger numbers. This is because the Fortress Model is not a set of bare minimums. Instead, it is what is required to 100% protect you from what is coming. If the numbers you see discourage you, don't worry. As I said earlier in this book, you have a good ten years (or so) to hit these benchmarks if you haven't yet.

So it's time to get to work. Here are the eight components of the Fortress Model. They are not listed in any particular order and all eight are required.

Fortress Model Component 1:
Inner Circle of Fortifying People Who Love You

Surprised you, didn't I? You were probably expecting the first item to be some financial amount of money you need or the types of investments you should have. Don't worry, we'll get there, but not yet.

My job here is to give you a 100% comprehensive plan that protects you completely. The scientific data is very clear that the emotional component is just as important to your long-term well-being as external components like business, internationalizing, and money. The data is also very clear that if you have people in your life who love you, that can be just as impactful and important as having a high income or net worth (though you need that money stuff too).

However, while I need to be comprehensive I also need to be objective and rational. This means that having "people who love you in your life" is not enough. As a matter of fact, the common advice of "having people in your life who love you" actually gets a lot of people in trouble and causes a lot of chronic stress, problems, and unhappiness. I shall explain.

By "love" in this context, I mean any kind of love from another human being. It can be romantic love, family love (siblings, parents, kids, etc), or the love of close friends. And no, the love you get from your pets doesn't count. I adore dogs and cats but the data clearly shows your dog loving you is no substitute for the love from another human.

If No One Loves You

If you currently have literally no one in your life who loves you, meaning you have no close relationship with either of your parents, and you have no close friends, no close siblings, no children, and no romantic partners (hookers don't count, sorry), then that's a problem you need to solve. Guarding yourself against the Creeping Darkness and the AI Black Hole of Unknown is going to take a decent amount of time, effort, and focus, both when you're building your Fortress and when you're actually experiencing the collapse of the West or the Ten Years of Brutality. If you have no emotional support during these times, if you're feeling sad, lonely, alienated, touchy, angry, depressed, or just all-around shitty because you don't have anyone who loves you, you're far more likely to fail no matter how well you do financially or internationally.

"But I'm an introvert!" you say.

Yeah, great, so am I. I'm Myers Briggs INTJ and I'm a pretty hardcore introvert myself. Doesn't matter. Introverts need love just as much as extroverts. Just because you're an introvert doesn't mean you're not human. So I'm sorry, but that's *not* an excuse.

If you are very introverted it perhaps is true that you need *fewer people* in your inner circle of people who love you. The extrovert might need eight or nine people in his inner circle and you the quiet introvert might just need two, and that's fine, but two is not zero. Two is two, and if you have zero you need to go get your two instead of making bullshit excuses about having zero.

How do you go about getting more people in your life who love you? Unfortunately, things like dating skills, parenting skills, how to find close friends, and relationship skills are huge and vast topics well outside of the scope of this book. One of my companies is teaching men dating and relationship skills so you're welcome to go to AlphaMale20.com for some resources on that if you're a man. You have access to the internet and thousands of books on these topics; go do some research and get this done. It might take you a year or two to do so; that's fine. Perhaps just two or three people in your inner circle is all you need.

If Draining People Love You

It's much more likely that you indeed have several people who love you already. That's great, but you're not done, and this part of your Fortress is still not built.

All the people who love you, regardless of the type of love, be they your mom, long-time buddy, girlfriend, or whomever, fall into one of two categories:

- People who love you who *drain* you
- People who love you who *fortify* you

I hate to tell you this, and this is something not a lot of people like to talk about, but not all of the people who love you fortify you. Not all the people who love you are good for you. We generally assume that if someone loves us, that's good and we can just move on. Incorrect. Many people who love you can actually be draining you instead of making you stronger, happier, and more motivated. These drainers are quite literally poisonous; they're killing you slowly.

There are three types of draining people who love you.

The first type of person drains your *emotions*. They love you, and maybe you love them, but they're *exhausting*. After a conversation with them, you feel like you've just run a marathon. They pull your focus away from your life, safety, happiness, and future and instead point it all to them and their problems. They argue with you often. They complain often. They make demands or requests of you often. They're negative all the time. They're just a big damn pain in the ass!

If you have any emotional drainers in your life, you already know exactly who they are. As soon as you read the last paragraph you were nodding your head and thinking about them. ("Yep, that's mom!")

The second type of person drains your *money*. Maybe they're perfectly nice people who don't cause you any emotional stress or drainage, but they cost you real money that you have to sink into them every month. Instead of putting that money where it belongs, like in your skill growth, location-independent business, cash reserves, or investments, you give it to them. And here's the thing; *they don't necessarily need it*. To be clear, a money drainer is not any person who loves you and costs you any money. If you have small children they need your financial support so they're obviously okay and don't fall into this category. The same would go for your wife if you're a man who has a loving, happy, stay-at-home wife taking care of your kids and/or your household; again, she costs you money but the cost is acceptable.

I'm talking about people such as:

- The hot but high-maintenance girlfriend who is constantly pushing you to buy her more expensive gifts and lifestyle trappings.
- The long-time loser friend who is always asking you for money to help him out of a jam (which is always his fault) promising that this time will be the last time he asks, which you know isn't true.
- The old, retired mother who is constantly calling you and complaining about her various problems and guilt-tripping you if you don't help her out with some money.
- The bitchy wife who demands you spend hundreds or even thousands of dollars on your kids by buying them a mountain of toys, fancy parties, or other stupid ass-kissing or helicopter-parenting bullshit.

Like I said above, you know who these people are in your life and who they are not.

The third type of person is the worst one of them all. This is the person who drains both your emotions *and* your money. These super-drainers are truly toxic to your life, well-being, and future.

Now here's the problem, and I can already hear your brain thinking this: "Yeah, okay, my mom is definitely draining on my emotions and my money, but c'mon man. She's my mom! I can't just cut her out of my life!" Then you come up with all the bullshit excuses. "I mean, she's 67 years old and fat and suffers from depression and has a bad back. Who else is going to take care of her? My dad is dead and my brother's an asshole so he's not going to do it. I mean, yeah, she's a bitch from hell and I have to send her my hard-earned money all the time which I can barely afford, but if I don't send her money and listen to her complain about her life and how I'm a bad son all the time, she could... uh... I don't know... die or something!!!"

If you have thoughts like this about any drainers in your life, you need to go look up the term "co-dependent." Actually, fuck it, I'll do it for you right now. Here it is:

Co-dependent refers to a type of relationship where one person has an excessive emotional or psychological reliance on another person, typically to the detriment of both individuals. In co-dependent relationships, one person often enables or supports the unhealthy behaviors of the other, while neglecting their own needs and well-being. This dynamic can occur in various types of relationships, such as romantic, familial, or friendships.

Yeah, does that sound familiar? That's you. It's time for you to stop this bullshit and grow up.

Here's the bottom line, and I'm being very serious about this. You will not survive what is coming if you have drainers in your inner circle. Period, end of story. You won't be able to A) do what's necessary to prepare and B) survive what will come once it does come. It's like fighting off a room full of orcs with your sword while there's two vampires on your back sucking out your blood at the same time. While you're busy making excuses about how much the vampires love you, you get weaker and weaker. Then you're so weak you drop your sword and the orcs chop your head off. Then they kill the vampires too. Well done.

All drainers in your loving inner circle must be either ejected from your life or the relationship needs to radically change so that they don't drain your emotions or money anymore (which is unlikely; usually they'll have to be ejected). I don't like that any more than you do. Doesn't matter. It must be done if you want to survive what's coming.

If you're a man, I strongly recommend my primary book, The Unchained Man, which will help you with difficult decisions like this.

If Fortifying People Love You

If you have people who love you, once you've ejected the drainers from the group, or were lucky enough to not have any drainers there in the first place, congratulations. You now have an inner circle of people who fortify you. These are people who not only love you, but are positive influences on your life. They build you up, encourage you, and/or make you feel good. Maybe even some of them don't do anything overtly fulfilling, but they don't drain your emotions or money in any way and they fill you with a great desire to help them and be by their side. In other words, fortifying people motivate you and make you stronger.

You might be wondering what kind of configuration you need in this inner circle. Should you have X amount of family members, Y amount of friends, and Z amount of romantic partners? This is purely up to you based on your personality type, temperament, age, preferences, and family situation. Just like with the exact number of people in your loving inner circle, there is no right or wrong answer. Sit down and think about what the ideal configuration for you would be.

If it's exactly what you already have, great, this part of your Fortress is now built and you can continue to build the other parts listed in this chapter.

If it's close to what you have but not exactly, then just keep your eyes out for that missing person or persons. They'll come eventually.

If your ideal configuration isn't anything like you have now, then similar to the person who has no one, you need to get out there and bring these people in as fast as you're able, even if it takes a year or two. At least you've already got people who already support and motivate you.

Fortress Model Component 2:
A Location-Independent Alpha 2.0 Business

To be 100% free and protected from what is coming, you can't have a job working for someone else. Having a job was a perfectly fine thing back in 1965 or 1982 but today it's a path to financial suicide. People who rely on jobs to pay their bills are massively exposed to what is coming.

1. Having a job means you can be fired or laid off whenever your boss, boss's boss, company, or industry decides they don't need you anymore or can no longer afford you. This is not security.
2. Having a job means you can be laid off if there is any change in the marketplace, economy, or technology, all of which are coming (and to a large degree are already here).
3. Having a job, even if it's a remote job in most cases, means you are rooted in the city where you currently have that job. Likely, that city is in the Collapsing West. Being stuck in your current collapsing city to pay your bills is a terrible idea for numerous reasons I've already covered in this book.

4. Having a job means you have very little control over your day-to-day schedule.
5. Having a job means you have zero flexibility. You have no power whatsoever to change your working hours, schedule, what you're working on, who you work with, or where your money comes from. You're a slave.

Perhaps you don't have a job but instead rely on gigs for your income. Gigs would be things like being a driver for rideshare services, a delivery driver for online food delivery services, or doing freelance work on services like Upwork. While this is slightly less bad than having a typical 9-5 job, it's still a serious problem. You're (likely) location-dependent on your local city, your income is always unpredictable, your income is determined by your host companies (who can change how you get paid at any time, and often do), and technology like AI will wipe out most or all of your gigs in the next few years (try being an Uber driver when driverless cars are commonplace).

Perhaps you do have your own business, but it's a location-dependent business where you must physically be present to service your customers or clients in your local city. Today, this is as bad as having a job. If there are any problems in your current collapsing Western city (which there will be), any economic problems, any changes in the law, or any collapse scenarios there, you're going to lose your entire company and then be forced to start all over again from scratch. Moreover, you're likely paying ridiculous amounts of taxes to your local, state/provincial, and federal governments. All bad.

The solution to all of these problems is to have your own business that is 100% location-independent.

Historically it was more risky to have your own business than having a job. In the last 15 years or so, this has reversed. Today people with their own businesses are actually safer than people with jobs. Let's compare the above list to the person who has their own location-independent business instead of having a job, many of which also apply to if you rely on gigs or a location-dependent business.

1. When you have your own location-dependent business, no one can fire you. You could lose a customer here or there and that happens all the time, but losing a few customers doesn't mean your entire company shuts down; your income continues.

2. When you have your own location-dependent business, no one can lay you off. If there is a sudden sharp change in the marketplace, economy, or technology, instead of suddenly losing 100% of your income like people with jobs who get fired or laid off, you can do something job-holders can't: you can *pivot*. You can quickly change what your business is doing and/or how it's doing it and maintain your business and your income. I've been consistently self-employed for almost 30 years and I've done pivots like this at least six times; it's no big deal.

3. When you have your own location-dependent business, you can travel to, visit, or live in any place in the world you want, stay there for as long as you want, and the income just keeps coming. You're not stuck or wedded to any one country, collapsing or otherwise. You can travel and live literally wherever you want and the money keeps dropping into your checking account. It's awesome.

4. When you have your own location-dependent business you set your daily schedule. You work whenever you want and play whenever you want.

5. When you have your own location-dependent business you have *massive* flexibility. At any time you can change your hours, schedule, what you're working on, who you work with, or where the money comes from. It's all up to you.

I have been teaching something called the Alpha 2.0 Business Model for almost 15 years. It is a specific type of business that provides you the most amount of freedom and security more than any other type of business you could own. The Alpha 2.0 Business provides the most amount of income on the least amount of hours worked, as quickly as possible, while offering the owner the most amount of personal freedom, mobility, and long-term safety.

Here are the ten parameters of an Alpha 2.0 Business.

1. The Alpha 2.0 Business is 100% location-independent.

This means that the business, all of your customers/clients, and all of your vendors do not care where you are located. You can travel anywhere in the world and stay there as long as you want, even months or years, and you have zero dip in your income from your Alpha 2.0 business.

If you have to be physically located somewhere specific to maintain your income, to service your customers, or to get new customers, your business doesn't qualify as Alpha 2.0 and it won't protect you for the long term.

2. The Alpha 2.0 Business has zero employees.

The vast majority of people who own businesses with employees are not free. It's often just as bad as having a job with a boss; sometimes it's even worse. By "employees" I'm referring to W-2 salaried employees or the non-American equivalent if you live outside of the USA. Utilizing help from virtual assistants, subcontractors, temporary workers, volunteers, interns, consultants, coaches, or advisors is all okay and usually necessary. My largest company has 22 people in it assisting me, but none of them are employees.

The problem with having employees is that your collapsing Western government will dictate to you how you manage them, how you hire them, how much you pay them, how much benefits to give them, how much to tax them, and how you fire them. This means that *when you have employees you are co-running your company with your government.* You aren't in charge of your business, you and your government are. This is bad enough, but as we've already discussed, your government is going to get more oppressive and difficult to work with as it gets closer to collapse.

When you have no employees but use contractors and/or vendors instead, you are now 100% in charge. You can hire, fire, manage, and otherwise dictate how these people work with you. Big Daddy Government isn't constantly watching over your shoulder.

3. The Alpha 2.0 Business is profitable within 90 days (or so) of starting it.

There are lots of online or location-independent businesses that are perfectly fine business models but when you start them from scratch they take way, *way* too long before you get a lot of money in your pocket as profit. Starting a business like developing an app, having a SAAS company, writing an ebook, or becoming an influencer are all perfectly fine, but it's going to take you a year or even several years before you as the business owner makes any real money.

The Alpha 2.0 Business makes you money fast, within 90 days, so you can quit your horrible 9-5 job and get free ASAP. In our 90 Day Business Builder Program we have people regularly start their first business, having never started one before, and get customers that pay them anywhere from $8,000 to $50,000 in just a few weeks. Now *that's* a business! If you want to do stuff like develop an app or course, or write a book, that's fine, do that as your second income stream or business, once your first income stream is making you money and you've quit your job and become location-independent.

4. The Alpha 2.0 Business is highly niched.

If you want to go out of business fast, offer a product or service to anyone on planet Earth. Like showing people how to lose weight (everyone needs to lose weight) or how anyone can save money (everyone needs to save money). You'll be out of business within a few weeks.

However, if you only offer your product or service to a very tiny, narrow niche, then:

- You will make more money.
- You will make it faster.
- You can charge more money for your products and services.
- You will need fewer customers to hit your financial goals.
- You will get more word-of-mouth referrals.
- You won't have to work as many hours.
- You'll be perceived as an expert much faster and sooner.
- It will be easier to target your marketing.

This is a win/win across the board. The Alpha 2.0 Business focuses on as narrow a niche as humanly possible rather than trying to help a billion people or a billion companies solve a common problem. (And again, if you *want* to be the next Elon Musk or Jeff Bezos and make billions of dollars selling stuff to billions of people, great, do that *after* you've started your Alpha 2.0 Business, quit your 9-5 job, and built your Fortress.)

5. The Alpha 2.0 Business always provides a flexible schedule for the owner.

This doesn't mean you can never schedule appointments or meetings. It means that if you have to constantly report to a certain company, person, or people at specific times not of your choosing, it's not an Alpha 2.0 business. The Alpha 2.0 Business owner can sleep in until 11 AM if he wants, and he can work or take time off whenever the hell he feels like it, while still making money and without having to check in with anyone.

6. The Alpha 2.0 Business only sells high-margin products or services.

"Margin" is the difference between your costs and how much you sell your product or service. Low-margin businesses are extremely difficult to run, scale, and make money from. The lower the margins are for what you sell, the more widgets you need to sell, the harder you have to work, the more marketing you have to do, the longer it takes to make money, the more staff you have to hire, the riskier your business is, and the more infrastructure your business requires. All bad.

I get offered businesses and business deals all the time. One of the first questions I ask is, "What are your margins?" If I get an answer like 5%, 15%, or 27%, I laugh and hang up the phone. I'm not going to work that hard, thank you very much.

The Alpha 2.0 Business has margins that are *at least* 300%, preferably 1,000%, 5,000%, or even more. If you have a mature business and a larger product line then it's okay if some of your products have margins that are lower than that, but the bulk of what you're doing has margins well past 300%. Examples of high-margin businesses would be coaching, consulting, and services. With margins like these, you only need a tiny amount of customers to make a lot of money. This means you work less while earning more. Speaking of working less…

7. The Alpha 2.0 Business doesn't require more than 30 hours per week of work to maintain once it's fully up and running.

A business owner who has to work 40, 50, or 60+ hours per week to maintain his income isn't free no matter how much money he makes. He might as well get a job. I'd rather have an Alpha 2.0 Business that pays me $100,000 a year than have a 50-hour-per-week location-dependent business that pays me $2 million a year.

The Alpha 2.0 Business does not require more than 30 hours a week to maintain once set up. The only possible exception to this is during the initial start-up period of the business, but's a temporary period only.

8. The Alpha 2.0 Business is AI-resistant.

With the Ten Years of Brutality and the AI Black Hole of Unknown looming over us, it doesn't make any sense to do things like open an accounting firm or legal research company or become a copywriter. In just a few years (or less) AI will replace everything you do, you'll be out of business, and you'll be one of the millions of starving victims of the Ten Years of Brutality. Stupid.

Instead, your business needs to be *AI-resistant*. This means that your business will either *never* be replaced by AI or worst case, if the AI Communist Utopia occurs, your business will be *one of the last ones on Earth* to be replaced (last man standing).

This means your business needs to include elements of one or more of the following:

- Highly creative problem-solving
- Highly creative strategic planning
- Highly creative and complex decision making
- High emotional intelligence
- Complex interpersonal interactions
- Extremely niched
- Mentorship and/or leadership
- Trust-based relationships
- High-touch services

With elements like those, you will not have to worry about AI replacing your business any time soon, or ever.

9. The Alpha 2.0 Business is 100% owned by you and no one else.

This means that you can't have any investors or equity partners of any kind in your Alpha 2.0 Business. No going into business with your best friend, girlfriend, or dad. Having investors can be just as bad as having a boss, and having partners is often even worse. I've seen many real-life horror stories of people doing great in business only to have a sudden catastrophe because of a partner's screw-up, change of heart, crimes, divorce, health problems, death, or other challenges completely outside of the owner's control. As the Western world continues to collapse, problems like this are going to increase, meaning having any partner equals increased odds of these issues occurring.

That being said, there can be exceptions to this rule. Sometimes investors or partners may be required on a short or medium-term basis, such as real estate investing or in a start-up, where you plan on selling your stock or ownership and exiting within a few years. I'm also not saying you should never rely on other people in your business; you can and probably should. My point is that these people don't need to own an equity share in your company. They can have their own separate company and you can pay them as a subcontractor.

10. The Alpha 2.0 Business can't be in any heavily regulated industry.

Having a business where you have to work with governments, government contractors, banks, attorneys, extremely complex science or technology, and similar entities is going to involve a lot of regulations, limitations on your operations, paperwork, time overhead, bullshit, and risk. Your Alpha 2.0 Business should be in a completely unregulated industry so you can run it the way you choose instead of how your government wants you to run it.

Fortress Model Component 3:
Fortress Income

As we already established, you need money to survive and thrive during the Creeping Darkness and the AI Black Hole of Unknown. It doesn't matter how lazy you are, how scared you are to start a business, how much you consider money "not that important," how left-wing you are, or how much you hate wealthy influencers on the internet. If you have little or no money, you will have pretty much zero options both now and later when these problems arise, which means you will be among the first people to be crushed by what's coming.

You must have money both in terms of income and net worth, and you're going to need more money than is what is considered average. I'm going to give you several numbers throughout the rest of this chapter, and if you're thinking they're too high or that I'm being unreasonable, remember that average people of average incomes are the ones who are going to be most negatively affected by Western collapse and AI. People who have money will either be 100% okay or at least much less bad off.

There are four money components to building your Fortress:

- Fortress Income
- Fortress Taxes
- Fortress Net Worth
- Fortress Cash

I'll cover Fortress Income right now and the other three below.

In my other books, I have said that the minimum income for long-term happiness is $85,000 USD per year or the equivalent in your local currency if you don't live in the Collapsing USA. This is based on numerous happiness studies over the past several years that empirically show that people who make less than $85K/year are less happy than people who make at least that amount or more. I have also said in the past that making more than this was optional based on your personality. Some people would be perfectly fine making $85K/year for the rest of their lives, while other people would be unhappy with that and would rather make $100K, $250K, $500K, $1 million, or more per year.

But now, the collapse of the Western world is upon us and the AI Black Hole of Unknown is rapidly approaching. This means $85K/year isn't going to cut it for most people. You're probably going to need more.

Fortress Income means you make between $85,000 to $250,000 per year before taxes or more. "Or more" is highly recommended, if you have the desire and energy to do it. The more you make, the safer you will be, *so there is no maximum to Fortress Income.* There is only the minimum range of $85K-$250K. This means you make at least $7K to $21K per month as net income from your business but before you pay any taxes (we'll cover taxes in a minute).

If you think this is a lot of money, let me remind you of a few facts.

1. Western Collapse, the AI Black Hole of Unknown, and the elites who are destroying the world don't give a shit about your feelings or opinions regarding what is or is not a lot of money. The more money you make the safer you will be with what's coming, and that's a fact regardless of your personal touchy feelings about it. Sometimes in life, you just need to suck it up. This is one of those times.

2. With today's skyrocketing inflation rates, $85K-$250K per year is not as much as you think it is. It might sound like a lot of money, but that's only because the software in your head is outdated. That *was* a lot of money 20 years ago. Not anymore. It's a much more achievable goal now.

3. If you follow all the Alpha 2.0 Business requirements I laid out above, making this kind of income isn't difficult. It's only difficult for you *now* because you have a stupid 9-5 job or you rely on gigs or a location-dependent business. Yeah, within your current context, $85K-$250K might sound like a lot of money, but if you start your own Alpha 2.0 Business and follow that structure, you'll be in a completely new context. The Alpha 2.0 blueprint has been tried and tested over the past 15 years and we know for a fact it works. We have complete beginners, people who have never had a business in their lives, in our 90 Day Business Builder program and our other programs get to $85K/year or more within just a few months by getting literally just three or four clients following this model.

You'll notice that $85K-$250K is a range, not an exact figure. The exact figure is something you're going to have to determine yourself based on a few parameters that I'll list in a minute. This is because everyone is in a different lifestyle scenario, so it wouldn't make any sense for me to just pick a single number and assign it to everyone in the world.

Here's how you determine your precise Fortress Income number. First, you need to determine which category you're in: *motivated* or *unsure*.

If, when you first read that $85K-$250K figure, your first thought was something like, "Pssh! That's all??? Hell, I want to make way more than that!!!" that means you're in the *motivated* category. If this is you, and you want to make more than $250K/year, then you need to make a spreadsheet list of everything you want in life and attach real monthly costs to each of these items. What kind of house do you want? What kind of car or cars do you want? If you want or have kids, how much money do you want to provide them with? List everything. When I did this, I put down things like regular business class airline flights, weekly massages, dream homes in two different countries, and so on, with exact numbers attached to each.

Add up all of the numbers, and boom, there's your monthly income goal which is probably more than $21,000. Great, that is now your Fortress Income. Now get to work!

(Note: If you want to do the extra-hard advanced version of this, you can do what I did when I did this several years ago. Once I determined my magic income number, *I doubled it* and *that* became my number. I did that because I wanted to account for inflation and any changes in lifestyle or preferences that may have occurred in my life between when I set the goal and when I hit the goal. But I'm a highly motivated workaholic manic with a strong mission in life, so this is purely optional for you. Alternatively, you could add 20% or something to your number just to be safe. Again, it's completely up to you.)

On the other hand, if when you first read that $85K-$250K per year figure, your first thought was something like, "Wait… what??? This guy seriously thinks I need to make THAT MUCH MONEY??? That's just crazy. There's no way I could make that much!" or even if your first thought was something like, "Wow, I don't know if I could make that much money, that sounds like a lot," this means you're in the *unsure* category. You need to follow a different process than the motivated people.

What you need to do is sit down and write or type out "$85,000 per year to $250,000 per year" at the top of a blank piece of paper or computer document. You now need to pick a number that is between $85K and $250K, and no, you can't just pick the lowest number because that may not be accurate. Instead, choose your best guess number of what you will want or need, *and be honest.* Then go through the numbered steps below, where you will modify this number up or down based on several factors. When it says "increase" or "decrease" the number, use your best guess as to how much this increase or decrease should be for you, just make sure you increase it or decrease it by a significant amount (not like $100 or something).

Also, the rules are that when it says you need to increase the number, you *must* increase it, but if it says you may decrease the number, you don't have to if you don't want to. Again, the higher this number ends up being, the better for you and your loved ones long-term. Also, the number can absolutely go past $250,000 per year if needed, so keep that in mind as you go through this exercise.

One quick note; if you don't live in the Collapsing USA, the convert this number from US Dollars to your own currency.

1. If you live in the Collapsing West, you must increase the number. The Western world is the most expensive place in the world to live in, by far, in terms of taxes, cost of living, and inflation. If you live outside of the West, you can reduce the number. If you live somewhere really cheap like Paraguay, you can *really* reduce the number. If you live in the Collapsing West and you live in a hyper-expensive city like New York or London, you need to increase the number even more.

2. If you plan on moving out of the Collapsing West to a cheaper country at some point in the next few years and you have a real plan to do this, you can reduce the number. If instead, you plan on staying in the Collapsing West for the rest of your life or even for the foreseeable future (God help you) then keep the number the same.

3. If you are under age 35, you may reduce the number. If you are age 50 or over, increase the number. Older people have less time to make more money, tend to have more financial responsibilities, and need money to take care of them in their very old age which is closer to them than it is for younger people.

4. If you have zero debt, you can decrease the number a little. If you have massive amounts of debt, increase the number. If you have a moderate amount of debt you may keep it the same or increase it a little.

5. If you have any children under the age of 25, increase the number. If you have no children but plan on having kids at any time in the future, increase the number. If you have no kids and you're *100% sure* that you'll *never* have any, or if you have kids but your youngest child is over the age of 25, you may decrease the number.

6. If you have a spouse or long-term significant other, increase the number, yes, even if this person has their own income. If you are single but plan on having a person like this in your life at some point in the future,

increase the number. If you are single (or single and dating someone) but you know for *100% sure* you will *never* live with a spouse or live-in boyfriend/girlfriend (which you realize is statistically unlikely), you may decrease the number.

7. If you are a very flexible person in terms of your lifestyle and are happy no matter what your living arrangements are, you may decrease the number. For example, I am like this. I am perfectly happy living in a multimillion-dollar home in a gated community and I'm just as happy living in a tiny one-bedroom apartment. However, a lot of people are not like this, so you need to be very honest with yourself. If you're more picky about exactly how your lifestyle needs to be arrayed, increase the number. (FYI, we're going to discuss your level of flexibility and the affect it will have on your international life in great detail later in this book.)

8. Lastly, increase the number if your gut feelings about the future are negative and you feel the number needs increasing, or if the number looks too small to you. To repeat yet again, the higher this number, the better, and it can go well past $250,000 if necessary. There is no maximum!

Feel free to do this exercise two or three times before you have it nailed down. Once you do, convert the annual number to a monthly income number (divide by twelve), and boom, there's your monthly Fortress Income number that you must hit. Your Fortress is not built until you start earning this figure. The later chapters in this book will help you hit that number, so don't worry.

Fortress Model Component 4:
Fortress Taxes

As I've shown in prior chapters, the typical modern-day Westerner pays around 51% to 70% of his total income in some form of tax to his government. To repeat and be clear, some of these taxes are taxes you see, like when your employer takes payroll or income taxes out of your paycheck or when you pay a sales tax at the grocery store. Some of these taxes are taxes you don't see, like when you pay your rent, much of that is property taxes but you don't see it.

I could now go on a big libertarian political rant about how paying these exorbitant tax rates is absolutely ridiculous under any conditions, but they're even worse considering that you get virtually nothing of value in return (limited social services, roads and bridges that get worse every year, prices that go up every year, billions of tax dollars sent to other countries, millionaires, people who can work but choose not to, etc) and how this kind of taxation is literally is theft and immoral, and so on, but I won't do that. This book is not about political opinions; it's a book about tactics and facts.

Instead, the key points regarding how much taxes you pay that have nothing to do with left, right, or libertarian politics are the following:

1. You can't afford to pay these tax rates with what's coming. If you lived in a financially strong, booming economy and thriving culture with a bright future over the 50 years with no AI on the horizon at all, then I suppose it *might* be okay to pay a staggering 51-70% of your income to your government that just wastes the vast majority of it. Some Americans back in the 1950s paid these kinds of tax rates, but back then it was perfectly fine to do so. None of that is the case today. Even if you made $200,000 a year, for the government to take 60% of that ($120,000) leaving you just $80K for yourself and your family to prepare for, live, and thrive during the collapse of the West, the Ten Years of Brutality, and the possible AI Communist Utopia just isn't going to cut it. Not even close!

   I suppose if you made $2 million a year and paid half of that to the government leaving you with $1 million left over, you might be okay, but do you make $2 million a year? If not, are you going to make $2 million a year very soon? Maybe, but likely you're not going to make anywhere near this.

   You need Fortress Income *combined* with a very low tax rate. Just having Fortress Income and paying standard Western tax rates will *not* save you.

2. When you pay tax rates that high (51-70%), your government has a huge amount of access to your finances, bank accounts, investments, assets, and financial transactions. You're essentially in bed with your collapsing, corrupt, bankrupt, quasi-socialist, quasi-fascist, corporate-controlled government. In the era of Western Collapse, this is the opposite of what you want. You want your government(s) to have the absolute minimum access and control over your finances, assets, and doings.

   Over the next few years as Western governments run out of money, they're going to start doing some horrible things, including but not limited to "bail-ins" where they take money out of your bank account without your permission. If you think "that would never happen," it's already happened in Ireland, Cyprus, Poland, Italy, Spain, Netherlands, Denmark, and many other countries, and it will happen again.

Bail-ins is just one example; there are many other scary things your government can and will do to you as the collapse gets worse, and the more shared information and links you have to your collapsing Western government, the more likely these things are going to happen to you.

You probably pay 51-70% of your income in some form of tax to one or more governments. I pay around 5%. Who do you think is more exposed to these kinds of problems, you or me? Be honest.

3. Building your Fortress will take work, perhaps even a lot of work. Paying ultra-high tax rates means you're working harder for less money. Let's take the hypothetical guy who makes $2 million a year but pays 50% of that in taxes to his Western government. This guy is probably working extremely hard and long hours. He's working the hours necessary to earn $2 million but he's only getting $1 million. Does that make any sense to you? Because it doesn't to me. I'd rather work half the hours and make $1 million instead of $2 million. But see, unless he internationalizes he can't even do that. If he worked half the hours he'd make $1 million but the government would take half, meaning he'd have $500K left over, so he'd still be working double the hours necessary for that money.

If you're a psycho-workaholic and love working 60+ hours per week for fun and if you didn't have the Creeping Darkness and the AI Black Hole of Unknown right around the corner, then I guess do whatever you want and pay all the taxes you like, but again, that's probably not the scenario you're in. You need to free up as much time as you possibly can so you can build your Fortress and be protected from what's coming, as well as live a great life.

This all means you need to pay Fortress Taxes, not typical Western taxes. This means you must only pay a maximum of 15% total taxes on your entire annual income and do so legally without breaking any laws whatsoever. If you're paying more than that, and you probably are right now, you're exposed.

As I've mentioned, I pay around 5% in total taxes most years because of my international lifestyle. I know a lot of people who pay 2%, 1%, and a few who even pay zero percent, all completely legally, because of their international lifestyles. And of course, I know people who pay 8%, 10%, 12% and so on, well under our 15% threshold.

Can you legally reduce your overall tax burden without internationalizing at all? Of course you can; there are many techniques to do so. Can you legally reduce your overall tax burden to under 15% without internationalizing? If you're very poor and stay poor forever (meaning you're going to get crushed by what's coming) then yes. But if you make Fortress Income, no, you can't (unless your situation is very unusual).

This means you're going to have to internationalize in some way; you don't have a choice. You need to initiate at least Level 1 of internationalization we talked about back in the prior chapter, which is Offshoring. Otherwise, you're going to have to relocate under Levels 2 or 4. I don't know what your specific financial situation is so I can't tell you exactly what you need to do. It will depend on your income, the country where you live, your tax status, your net worth, whether you have a job or a business, how many kids you have, and many other factors. I'm just saying that getting your taxes below 15% overall is very likely going to require you to internationalize whether you want to or not. Later in this book, I'll show you how.

Fortress Model Component 5:
Fortress Net Worth

We've covered your business, your income, and your taxes. Now we need to address the next financial component of your Fortress, which is your net worth.

Net worth, if you are not sure what that means, is how much money value is left over after you take everything your own (your assets) and deduct all of the money you owe to anyone (your debts). That positive (or negative) number left over is your net worth.

To be clear, net worth does *not* indicate how much money you have. Most people are mistaken about this. They think that just because someone is "a millionaire" because his net worth is $4 million that means he has a mountain of $4 million in cash and gold bars in a big pile in his basement like Scrooge McDuck. No, quite the opposite. Statistically speaking, that guy probably has $2.5 million of that as equity in his house, another $1 million (at best) as valued for his small location-dependent business, and perhaps $500K or so in a bunch of IRA/401K retirement accounts that he's not allowed to touch without incurring massive penalties and punitive taxes.

Yeah, his net worth is $4 million but the bastard probably has $330 in his checking account and that's about it. Remember the stat I quoted earlier that said that 38% of Americans who make *more* than $100,000 a year could *not* get their hands on $1,000 cash in an emergency? That's exactly how this happens. Most "millionaires" in the Collapsing West are asset-rich but cash-poor. (We'll address actual cash reserves in a minute.)

So net worth is not a magic bullet. It is simply another buffer between you and the dangers that we face.

As I've shown many times throughout this book, you're going to need money to survive, much less thrive during what is coming (and to a large degree, what is already here). If you have no money or very little money, you're going to get slaughtered (at least figuratively). Hell, if you have no or very little money, you're probably already feeling the effects of Western collapse right this minute (high taxes, prices getting higher, layoffs, reduced work benefits, etc).

This means you need money. Unfortunately, you're going to need what most people consider "a lot" of money.

If, when the West collapses or when the Ten Years of Brutality begins in earnest if you have a negative net worth or a small net worth (as in under $100,000 or so), you're basically fucked. Kiss your ass goodbye, I hope you have a benevolent wealthy relative or something.

If instead, you have a net worth of around $100,000 to about $2 million, I hate to say this, but you're still screwed. First, that money isn't real cash (i.e. liquid) as I just explained, so you probably can't access those funds unless you do something drastic like sell your house. Do you want to rely on selling your house for quick cash in the middle of a collapse? Probably not. Secondly, with today's inflation rates which are going to get worse as the collapse intensifies, $100K - $2 million is barely middle class. You're going to need more than that to truly be protected. You need Fortress Net Worth.

With all of that context, here is the definition of Fortress Net Worth: $2.5 million USD in net worth or more *not including* the value of your primary residence. This means that if you own your own home and have equity in it, you can't include that towards this $2.5 million figure. You need to have net assets (that means after debts are deducted) of $2.5 million outside of the value of your home. If you have multiple homes, that's fine, this rule only applies to your primary residence where you live most of the year. If you rent your home (or homes) like I do, none of this is relevant because you don't own your home.

$2.5 million not including your primary residence is *a bare minimum*. *Optimal* Fortress Net Worth would be closer to $6 million or $7 million. At

$10 million, you're what I would categorize as "wealthy" and at $30 million or more you're "very wealthy." The good news is that $10 million or $30 million isn't required to build your Fortress (though those amounts would more than take care of you and your loved ones forever, even during the collapse), but at least $2.5 million is.

If you think $2.5 million not including your primary residence is an insanely high number that you could never achieve, you need to go back up to the Fortress Income section and re-read the parts about how inflation and your Alpha 2.0 Business makes this number much easier to hit (which we will also talk about more later in this book), and about the part where you need to just suck it up and get to work instead of making a bunch of excuses. Also remember you have (perhaps) about ten years to make this money, which is a very doable goal even if you're starting from zero or negative net worth today. I'm not saying you need to be worth $2.5 million right this minute (though that would be nice), I'm saying you need to earn and save this money to build your Fortress, and you still have some time to do so. Not a lot of time, but some.

If you're one of those motivated folks who wants to be worth $10 million or more and get rich, that's great. Get your ass to work and get it done. It's a nice place to be, and you'll be more than protected at these net worth levels.

Here's an "extra credit" assignment if you want to be super hardcore about this. Just if you want, you can change Fortress Net Worth to $2.5 million or more not including your primary residence *and* not including the value of your business. This is better because most millionaires have their entire net worths, or close to it, in their companies. If you're Jeff Bezos or Mark Zuckerberg, that's fine. But if you're a normal human owning a business, even if it's a location-independent Alpha 2.0 Business that makes you a lot of money, many of these companies can't be sold or can only be partially sold. Others could only be sold on pennies on the dollar. Others could be sold at full price but it would take many years to do so.

So if you want to be a super-badass about this, set a net worth goal that is more than $2.5 million that is purely made up of investments, *not* your business and *not* your primary home. This is what I do. All of my net worth objectives do not include the value of my companies, even though I could sell some of my companies (or parts of them) for a decent amount. I consider my *company valuations* and my *portfolio net worth* as two separate numbers, not one big number I combine.

Fortress Model Component 6:
Fortress Cash

If your net worth doesn't represent exactly how much money you have, then what does? Easy. That's the amount of your liquid cash reserves. This is the amount of cash or cash equivalents you have right now. This means if I put a gun to your head and told you to give me $40,000 in cash in 48 hours, you could do it because you have the cash in the bank or something you could very quickly convert to cash, like cryptocurrency.

Fortress Income and Fortress Net Worth aren't enough to protect you. You also need Fortress Cash. Here's the definition of Fortress Cash:

1. You have six to twelve months or more of personal expenses in cash, ready to go at any time.
2. You also have three months or more of business expenses in cash, ready to go at any time.
3. "Cash" in this context is defined as any of the following:
   a. Cash in the bank, like money in a checking or savings account.
   b. Cash in a liquid money market account or similar that is *not* under any sort of government retirement scheme (like an IRA or 401k).
   c. Physical cash stored somewhere, like in a safe or in your mattress.
   d. Any stablecoin cryptocurrency that is not under any sort of government retirement scheme. Remember that I didn't say cryptocurrency; I said *stablecoins only*, like USD Coin, Tether USDT, or Paxos Gold; i.e. crypto pegged to or backed by a real asset. Bitcoin and Ethereum are great, but they don't count as real cash because they're too volatile; their value could drop in half tomorrow right when you need it.
   e. A line of credit you can draw upon whenever you want without having to get permission from any bank. This is the least safe form of cash for several reasons (the bank could close your line of credit if/when things get bad) but it does technically qualify.
4. Lastly, none of your Fortress Cash can be stored in any Western bank. It *can* be stored in a Western investment or brokerage firm if needed, like Fidelity in the USA or Hargreaves Lansdown in the UK. Also, if any crypto is used as Fortress Cash, it can't be stored in *any* exchange like Coinbase or Binance. It *must* be stored in a non-custodial wallet (hardware or software doesn't matter). You will likely need to use Western banks and/or crypto exchanges to conduct your financial affairs; that's okay. I'm just saying that anything in these entities can't be counted towards Fortress Cash.

Here's how you determine how much you need to have in Fortress Cash. Add all the money you need to live per month. Don't include taxes but include everything else, all bills, debts, payments, food, automotive upkeep, if you support other people, etc. Be sure to include everything. Don't guess! If you're guessing, you're wrong. Instead, go back through your expenses (checking account statements if nothing else) for the past three months, divide it by three to get an average, and then use that figure.

Multiply that figure by six months, twelve months, or any other number more than six months. I like to have eight months of expenses in my cash reserves, but any amount is okay as long as it's at least six months.

Then, if you have a business, and hopefully you do because a location-independent Alpha 2.0 business is one of the Fortress requirements, do the same for all of your monthly business expenses, and multiply this amount by three months (or more if you wish). Add this amount to your total.

This total amount will be at least six months of personal expenses and three months of business expenses that you need to have in your cash reserves. Once you have this cash saved, now if you have any financial problems, even very serious ones, you have at least six months to figure it out before you have to start experiencing any severe repercussions. It makes you much more financially bulletproof. You are more than welcome to have twelve months of cash reserves or even more. It's completely up to you as long as you adhere to the six-month minimum for personal expenses and the three-month minimum for business expenses.

Here's an example of how Fortress Cash can help you, and the problems you will have if you don't have any.

Grant Cardone, who I generally like, has preached for years that "cash is trash" and that you should never have any cash and instead throw it into real estate as soon as you get any. Also for years, he bragged about how he had over 200 employees and made fun of people who had fewer employees than he did. This was all fine and dandy until the pandemic hit in 2020 (the worldwide overreaction to a flu with a 1% death rate). As soon as the lockdowns started, he immediately laid off 120 people from his company. This was despite the fact he was based in Florida where the lockdowns were the weakest in the USA. In a blink of an eye, he instantly wiped out almost two-thirds of his company, because he had no cash reserves of any kind. He experienced massive hate from the internet, infuriated 120 employees plus their families who were relying on him, and in my opinion, his brand permanently suffered because of it.

Here's the opposite example. Back when Bill Gates was CEO of Microsoft in the 1990s, he mandated that one year of Microsoft operating expenses always be held in cash in the bank. This way, he said, no matter what happened to Microsoft, the economy, or the world, they always had at least an entire year before they had to lay off even one person. Microsoft's annual operating expenses in the late 1990s were almost $6 billion. $6 billion in 1990s dollars in cash in the bank earning two or three percent interest? His advisors lost their minds! What a horrible way to allocate money! Bill stood firm though, and it worked. Back in 1999, it became one of the first companies in human history to hit a half-a-trillion-dollar market capitalization. Today it's worth over $3 trillion, making it the second largest company (as measured by market cap) in the world, larger than most *countries*.

The reason you don't want your Fortress Cash in any Western bank is because of the bail-in risk I explained earlier. You also don't want any of your cryptocurrency that you categorize as Fortress Cash in any exchange because the last ten years are rife with examples of people losing their crypto because of exchanges.

Non-Western banks are okay (as long as they're in stable countries like Singapore or the UAE) and Western brokerage firms are also acceptable because your odds of any bail-in problems with these entities are far less. It's also a good idea to spread your risk over two or three entities for your Fortress Cash. I would never have 100% of my Fortress Cash in one institution or crypto wallet.

If you're concerned that if you have all of this money in cash where you won't make a high-interest yield, you're right. Your cash reserve is not an *investment*, it's an *insurance policy*. If you only make half a percent interest on your cash, that's fine. Making interest on your Fortress Cash isn't the point. Having it there when you need it is the point. As Dan Pena once said, "I don't care about the return *on* my cash. I only care about the return *of* my cash." Exactly. If you want to make a higher rate of return, that's an investment that goes into your Fortress Net Worth, not your Fortress Cash.

If you're concerned that you have all of this cash in fiat currency (like dollars or euros) and that it will get murdered by inflation, then if you want to, as just an option, you can hedge some of this cash, say 20-30% with nonnumismatic gold coins. I said gold coins, not silver or any other precious metal. Feel free to do that if you'd like and if you're experienced in this area. Alternatively, you could add 3-7% to your Fortress Cash every year to account for things like inflation.

Personally, I don't worry about any of this with my Fortress Cash. These concerns are much more important for your Alpha 2.0 Business, Fortress Income, and Fortress Net Worth. Freaking about inflation or lack of interest on your Fortress Cash is stepping over dollars to pick up pennies in my view.

Fortress Model Component 7:
A Non-Western Base

This one should be pretty obvious by now. As part of your Fortress, you need to have a base of operations that is far outside of the Collapsing West. This protects you not only from Western Collapse but also increases your odds of surviving/thriving during the AI Black Hole of Unknown.

Having a non-Western base means one of two things:

Ideal: You don't live in a Western country. You can visit Western countries whenever you like and spend time there, but for the vast majority of the year, you live outside of the West.

Or…

Not ideal but acceptable: You live in a Western country but you have a fully-developed international backup plan exactly as I described back in Chapter 7.

So the good news is that you don't *need* to leave your collapsing Western country if you don't want to. At least not yet. You can stay in your collapsing Western nation but set up a non-Western international backup plan so you have somewhere to go when the shit hits the fan, which it will in your lifetime.

If you want extra credit on this part of your Fortress build, you can live in a non-Western country and still have an international non-Western backup plan to *that* country as well. This is what I have done. I live in the United Arab Emirates (Dubai), a happy, economically booming non-Western country, and I have a second home and residency in Paraguay, another economically booming non-Western country. Paraguay acts as a backup to Dubai just in case anything goes south with Dubai at any time in the future. It also works in reverse; Dubai acts as a backup to Paraguay in case anything goes wrong there.

I don't anticipate any future problems with either of these countries which is exactly why I chose them. The point is I've gone the extra mile in my Fortress to have a "backup to my backup," which makes me feel really good. I'm not only protected, I'm *super* protected.

Fortress Model Component 8:
Constant Supply of Emergency Necessities

This is the easiest step in building your Fortress. I first talked about this in my blogs back in 2017, years before the pandemic hit where it saved me and my wife a lot of pain and hassle.

You must always have in your home a minimum supply of the following items:

- Minimum 60 days' worth of emergency long-term nonperishable food per person who lives in your home. Often called emergency rations, you can get them on Amazon pretty easily and there is a wide selection.
- Minimum 60 gallons of clean water per person who lives in your home. This equates to two gallons per day for drinking, bathing, and cooking for a month.
- Minimum 30 days of disposable plates and bowls.
- Minimum 30 days of toilet paper and paper towels per person who lives in your home. This is always maintained, so as soon as you start getting down to 30 days left, *that's* when you go buy new toilet paper. You never wait to buy more when you're almost out like most people do.
- Minimum 60 days' supply of large heavy-duty trash bags.
- A small propane or butane-powered stove (often used for camping).

As I've explained earlier, I'm no doomsday prepper and I think most of those guys are a little too paranoid. That being said, having the above six items in constant supply just makes sense as a basic, prudent precaution. I personally know lots of people who were affected by a hurricane, flooding, massive snow storms, civil unrest in their city, long-term power outage, and similar who didn't have any of these things and they freaked the fuck out and experienced several weeks of severe pain and discomfort. During the pandemic (the worldwide overreaction to a flu with a 1% death rate) millions of people had panic attacks because the stores ran out of toilet paper and the like. Since my wife and I always maintained a 60-day minimum of that kind of thing in our home, we never worried once and never had a problem while all of our neighbors were losing their minds.

Also, none of this will ever be a waste of money because if you end up never using the food, for example, you just eat it before its expiration date. The same goes for the water and paper products.

Having these kinds of emergency necessities in your home has always been a good idea but today with the Creeping Darkness at our doorsteps and the AI Black Hole of Unknown just around the corner, it's now a 100% mandatory component of building your Fortress.

The Fortress Model Summarized

1. Several people in your life who love you and do *not* drain you of any emotions or money
2. A location-independent Alpha 2.0 Business
3. Fortress Income: $85K-$250K USD (or more) per year net profit before taxes from your business
4. Fortress Taxes: 15% total taxes or less (that includes *all* the taxes you pay) on your annual income
5. Fortress Net Worth: $2.5 million USD or more (ideally much more) not including your primary residence
6. Fortress Cash: At least 6 months or more of personal expenses and 3 months or more of business expenses in liquid cash
7. A non-Western base (you live outside of the West or have an international backup plan outside the West)
8. 60 days of emergency necessities at all times

Now that you understand what the Fortress Model is, for the rest of the book, we're going to talk about exactly how to build your Fortress.

Component #1 I've already discussed and component #8 is self-explanatory.

Components #2, #3, #5, and #6 are about making money through your Alpha 2.0 business. We'll cover that in detail in Part 3 of this book.

Components #4 and #7 are about protecting yourself and your money for the long term, minimizing expenses, and maximizing your freedom via an international lifestyle. We'll cover that in Part 4 of this book.

Part 3

How To Make Lots of Money While Remaining Free and Protected

Chapter 9

How To Start An Alpha 2.0 Business And Make Money In 90 Days Or Less

I'm about to give you precise instructions on how you can start your own Alpha 2.0-compatible business which will set you free, make you 100% location-independent, allow you to escape the Collapsing West, and eventually provide you with Fortress Income, Fortress Cash, and Fortress Net Worth.

I will also show you how to be profitable in 3-4 months or less. Many people in our 90 Day Business Builder program have gotten huge clients within this time frame starting from scratch with no business experience.

You can start this business on the side, in addition to your current job, and then quit your job as soon as your new business starts making consistent income. This is exactly how millions of people have started businesses like this, myself included.

Step 1: Set Aside At Least 15 Hours Per Week To Work On This

You don't need to quit your full-time job to start this business, but you will need at least 15 weekly hours. 15 hours is a minimum; 20 hours is better, and 30+ hours is even better. The more time you put into this per week, the faster the money and freedom will come.

Step 2: Determine A Very Narrow Niche

As I mentioned in the prior chapter, if you want to get from zero to the money fast, you only sell things to an extremely narrow niche and refuse to sell to anyone else. Selling to "anyone in the world who wants X" is extremely difficult, raises the odds of failure, and takes much longer to get to the money. If you really want to sell something to the entire world, you can always do that once you've built your Fortress. For now, to get free and profitable as fast as possible, you need to *niche*... and narrow as you can.

When I say this, people often worry that their niche might be "too small." **You can't niche too much!** Here's a true statistic from my life: I have never seen a tiny, narrow niche that wasn't big enough to make a seven-figure income from.

The more you niche:

- The easier it is to get customers.
- The higher prices you can charge.
- The more referral business you will get.
- The fewer customers you need to hit your income goals.
- The easier it is to locate prospects.
- The cheaper it is to advertise.
- The faster you will be perceived as an expert.
- The less competition you'll have.
- The less customer turnover you'll experience.
- The less hard you'll need to work for the equivalent income of the person who isn't niching.

With all of these massive advantages, it is literally stupid to not niche.

Most people don't understand what the word "niche" means. It means an extremely small and narrow segment deep within an industry or demographic. "Health care" is not a niche. That's an *industry*, and a huge one at that. Neither is "doctors," "lawyers, " "tech," or "fitness." These are not niches! These are massive, broad industries. Similarly, "single mothers" or "men between ages 25 and 45" are also not niches. These are broad *demographics*.

An example of a niche would be "podiatrists in private practice nearing retirement." Now *that's* a niche. See how specific and narrow that is instead of "doctors?" Another example would be "professional male piano players over the age of 45". That's a niche, rather than saying "musicians" or "middle-aged men," which are not niches.

Your niche can be a narrow type of individual (called business to consumer, or B2C) or a narrow type of business (called business to business, or B2B). Either is acceptable and I've made good money doing both. However, B2B is far superior to B2C in most cases. Here's why:

- Selling to businesses means it's going to be easier to determine the niche's problem (which is step 3 below).
- Selling to businesses means you can charge a lot more money (companies have a lot more money than individuals).
- Selling to businesses means you can create bigger improvements with more impact. There's quite a difference between saving an individual $7,000 and saving a company $2,000,000. This means more income for you and happier clients.

- Selling to businesses means you need fewer customers to hit your financial goals. This means less work for you for the same amount of money.
- Selling to businesses means you'll have fewer problematic clients who complain far less and ask for refunds far less.

Step 3: Uncover The Niche's Biggest Problem

Most new business owners look at themselves and what they're good at or what they like, and then project this out into the marketplace.

"I'm good at computers, therefore I'm going to sell computer services!"

"I lost a bunch of weight, therefore I'm going to help people lose weight!"

"I'm an accountant, therefore I'm going to help people with their accounting!"

This is usually a huge mistake and explains why more than 80% of new businesses fail quickly.

Instead, a much faster and safer way to make money quickly in a new business is to *find the niche's biggest problem and help them solve or alleviate that problem.* This is completely irrelevant to what you want to sell or do.

I know this is a difficult pill to swallow, but the reality is that no one gives a shit about you, your skills, your interests, or your experiences. These things can sometimes assist you, sure, but what people care about are their *own* problems, especially their biggest problem. *That* is what they'll spend good money to fix or improve.

Once you select your narrow niche, do some research and find out what your niche's biggest problem is. Email them, DM them, call them on the phone, and talk to them. Find out what bothers them, what they're angry about, what frustrates them, and/or what scares them.

If you speak with a bunch of people in your niche and start hearing the same problem repeated over and over again, bingo, that's their biggest problem. (Discovering their second biggest problem is also useful.)

What if you don't know how to solve their problem? No problem! You can contract hire specialists, technicians, admin people, or subcontractors online very inexpensively who know exactly how to solve the problem. You get the customer, get paid by the customer first, *then* pay your contractors to solve the problem, make sure they do a decent job, and then take the profit. And remember, Alpha 2.0 Businesses do not have any employees, so you don't actually hire any of these folks as such (though you can certainly use them on a long-term basis as a vendor or subcontractor).

Alternatively, you can help your niche solve their second biggest problem; often that works just as well. I would *not* start a business on a niche's third biggest problem or below that, however.

What if you can't fully solve their problem 100%? That's okay because you can probably *alleviate* it. Think about your current biggest problem in your life right now. If I couldn't solve that problem for you but I could alleviate it or improve it by 60%, would that be worth some money you'd pay me? Of course it would!

Step 4: Sell Coaching, Consulting, or A Service To Solve or Alleviate the Niche's Problem

There are lots of business models and lots of possible things to sell to customers to help them solve or alleviate their problems. Some of these are not Alpha 2.0 compatible and some are. However, even many Alpha 2.0 compatible business ideas are not good ideas for first-time businesses.

Remember from the Alpha 2.0 Business requirements in Chapter 8 that your business must make money fast (ideally within 90 days), be AI-resistant, and only sell high-margin items. Many good business models have some of these aspects but not all of them. This makes them not ideal for your first business.

For example, writing ebooks is fantastic and I've made millions selling books myself, but selling an ebook as your first business isn't a great plan because it's going to take you at least a year (at best) to outline it, research it, write the entire thing, proofread it, typeset it, getting on all of the sales platforms, and then market it. During that entire time, you're not making any money. Odds are you'll probably stop working on it because most people don't like putting in 12+ months of effort for zero pay.

Wouldn't you rather make several thousand dollars in 90 days or less? And perhaps quit your job in six months or less? You could honestly quit your job in half the time it would take you to write and self-publish an entire book. It's the same for things like selling hard products, selling online courses, developing an app, becoming famous on social media, and so on. These things are all great and I've done many of them myself, but the problem is that these things take a long time to get any real, reliable, net income. I'd rather see you make thousands of dollars in just a few weeks, and that's not going to happen with any of those ideas (barring unusual exceptions to the rule).

In addition, many business ideas touted today are low-margin, like selling lawnmowers online as a drop shipping company. These businesses require a lot of customers to make any decent money, which means more time, more marketing, more customer service staff you have to hire, and so on. They also tend to sell to consumers instead of businesses, which means you'll have to deal with more complaints and refund requests.

Instead, what you want to sell in your first Alpha 2.0 business is *coaching*, *consulting*, or a *service*.

Coaching means you advise people one-on-one or in very small groups, remotely of course.

Consulting means you advise companies and/or organizations. I made millions of dollars as a consultant for decades before I ever made one penny online.

A *service* means instead of telling your customers what to do via coaching or consulting, you just do it for them. You can sell a personal service (B2C) or a business service (B2B) (but again, B2B is better).

Here's why coaching, consulting, or a service is superior to all of the other possible things you can sell in a first-time business:

- It takes minimal planning or prep time. It might take you six months to develop an online course but it might only take you two days to plan out a profitable service.
- It directly addresses the niche's problem, which is exactly what they want.
- It's high-margin and high-markup, meaning the profitability and profit margin on what you sell is sky-high when compared to things like selling hard products or developing an app, where there are lots of costs you need to incur pre-sale and post-sale. You have none of these costs coaching or consulting, and very little selling a service, which means all or most of the profit goes right into your pocket.
- You don't have to do the work yourself if you don't want to. You can outsource the work to technicians, specialists, or administrative staff.
- You can do all of it 100% location-independently. All the work you perform as a coach, consultant, or service provider will be 100% remote.

If you want to sell things like courses, apps, ebooks, and so on, you still can! Start your coaching/consulting/service business *first*, make some money, get a customer base, perhaps get a social media following, quit your job, internationalize, get better at what you're doing, and *then* start selling courses, books, apps, and so on as new income streams. I did this and it worked very well.

You might be thinking that you could offer consulting/coaching *and* a service. Again, start with just one of those first. Get a few customers under your belt to get more comfortable with what you're doing, then add your second item. Keep things simple when you start a new business – just sell one thing first.

Step 5: Aggressively Market Your Service Via Paid or Free Methods

The final step is to tell everyone in your niche about what you're doing so they can buy from you. If you have no money, you can do this using free marketing methods such as:

- Social media
- Videos
- Blogging
- Podcast
- Articles
- Cold calls
- Cold DMs
- Forum outreach
- Networking with your warm contacts
- Joint ventures.

I started my online business back in 2009 for a total cost of $29. I didn't spend one penny on any paid marketing or ads until the business was already making six figures, so free marketing works as long as you're patient, narrowly niched, focused on the niche's problem, and put in the time.

If you have some money to spend, you can instead market using paid marketing methods by running ads online, paying telemarketers, or other forms of paid advertising. Since you are narrowly niched, these ads won't cost you nearly as much money as those people trying to sell something to the entire world.

Step 6: Quit Your 9-5 Job or Gigs When Your Business Reaches 40% Of Your Job/Gigs Income

Take a minute and calculate 40% of your current after-tax monthly job/gigs income. Whatever that number is, as soon as your new business makes that amount per month three months in a row, you can now quit your job. Congratulations, you're now free to move or travel to wherever you want and you've built a key component of your Fortress!

Why not wait until it makes 100% of your job income? Because when you quit your job/gigs, suddenly you now have an extra 40 or 50 hours per week to put into your business. This is more than enough time needed to make up that remaining 60%.

If you have a lot of money in liquid savings already, you could drop this 40% figure down to 30% or even 20%.

The beauty of this plan is because you're selling something high-margin to a narrow niche, you don't need very many customers to make a decent amount of money. People incorrectly assume you need hundreds or thousands of customers paying you money before you can quit your job. Under the Alpha 2.0 Business model, this is incorrect. As a consultant, you could possibly quit your job after getting just *two* clients. If you sell coaching or a service, you could possibly quit your job once you have perhaps 3-10 customers or less, that's it!

Making Your Business AI-Resistant

As we've already talked about, because of the Ten Years of Brutality and the AI Black Hole of Unknown bearing down upon us, the goal of your Alpha 2.0 Business is to either *never* be replaced by AI or at least be the last man standing if AI replaces everyone and be among the last people/businesses that AI replaces.

I gave you a list of traits of an AI-resistant business back in Chapter 8. Your job is to integrate as many of these elements as you can within the solutions you sell to your customers. Using myself as an example, my online business consists of myself and other real-life humans giving our clients hands-on advice and assistance that solves highly complex problems in a highly niched area using lots of high-touch services, mentorship, and trust-based relationships. If the AI Communist Utopia ever comes to pass, I will be literally one of the last people in the world replaced by AI. If the AI Communist Utopia never happens, then my business will *never* be replaced by AI even though many others will be.

In either scenario, my business will be *aided* by AI, enabling me to make more money, faster, cheaper and using less of my personal time. Honestly, instead of the Ten Years of Brutality scaring me, I'm quite excited about it because, during that time with my Alpha 2.0 Businesses and international lifestyle, my life is going to benefit greatly from the productivity gains of AI instead of being threatened by them.

You need to think the same way when you determine how to solve or alleviate your niche's problem.

Here's the great news: my advice above *already* makes your business AI-resistant. Having a coaching, consulting, or service-based business in a highly niched area already makes it difficult (though not impossible) to be replaced by AI. Just make sure that if you're a service-based business, your service involves a lot of high-touch, personalized, human service instead of a completely automated service that can be replaced by AI more quickly.

What If You Already Have A Business?

It's possible that you may already have a more traditional business of your own that isn't Alpha 2.0 compatible. Maybe it's a location-dependent business. Perhaps it's a location-independent business but you sell low-margin stuff, or it's not niched, or you have lots of employees.

If you already have your own business, there are only two questions that matter:

- Is it 100% location-independent?
- Does it make your Fortress Income, reliably, every year?

These are both yes or no questions. Don't tell me your business is "sort of" location-independent or that it "kind of" makes your Fortress Income.

Either you have to be physically located in a particular city over and over again to earn your money, or you don't. If you have the kind of business where sometimes (as in two or three times a year but not more) you need to go somewhere to put on a training session, onboard a new client, or do a seminar, then that's technically okay. If you have to be located somewhere more than that, it's a location-dependent business and you have some changes to make.

If your business makes your Fortress Income every year, reliably, then great. If it makes your Fortress Income some years but not others, or has made your Fortress Income one time, then you have some improvements to make.

Here's the breakdown based on the answers to those two questions:

- *It's location-independent and it makes your Fortress Income.* Congratulations, this part of your Fortress is now built and you can move on. The only thing you need to worry about is to ensure it's AI-resistant, but you have time to make those changes.
- *It's location-independent but it doesn't make your Fortress Income.* This means you need to scale your business. You need more customers/clients and you need to streamline your operations for maximum profitability. Start working on this immediately.

- *It's not location-independent but it makes your Fortress Income.* This means you need to convert your business to make it Alpha 2.0 compatible and location-independent. This is a complex topic and beyond the scope of this book. I would strongly suggest you go to calebjones.com or reach out to my team at theonlyblackdragon@gmail.com to find out how we can help you.

- *It's not location-independent and it doesn't make your Fortress Income.* This is a problem. This essentially means that your business is a liability to you and your future life. You need to start your Alpha 2.0 Business on the side just as if you had a 9-5 job and get that up and running as fast as you can. Then when your Alpha 2.0 business is making you a decent amount of money, you can scrap or sell your existing business and get your Fortress built. The good news is that you already have business experience so this won't be a very long process for you. You're also a good candidate for the 90 Day Business Builder program.

Questions and Answers

Here are the most common questions or concerns I get when I describe the process of setting up your Alpha 2.0 business, with their answers.

What if I pick the wrong niche or the wrong thing to sell?

Then, using the information you've gathered up until then, you pivot to a slightly different niche or slightly different thing to sell and keep moving forward. It's no big deal and happens to entrepreneurs all the time. Various times throughout my business career, I've tried to sell things to certain niches and I failed, but, and this is a big BUT, I always learned things from the process that helped me pivot to something else that *did* make me money very fast.

A few years ago I tried to sell my audience a line of NFTs. This failed; I jumped the gun too fast and my audience wasn't yet ready for the technology (but they will be soon, and then I'll launch NFTs again and it will work). However, during that entire process, I learned that my audience wanted a certain type of coaching program. Using what I learned from the failed NFT launch, I launched that program and made an almost immediate profit of $400,000. I also learned that my audience responds very well to adult-oriented comic books as a branding tool, so I have big plans to capitalize on that as well.

Failure always equals lots of money as long as you keep iterating, pivoting, and taking action.

Why would anyone hire me? I'm new/never done it before/don't know anything.

Several reasons. First, you're going to position yourself as someone who only works in their niche. This builds a lot of trust. Think about it if you were on the other side. Someone is trying to help you get a particular result and will help anyone who asks, versus someone who is doing the same thing but only works with people exactly like you, in your precise, specific situation. You'd be a lot more comfortable giving the second guy money than the first guy, right?

Secondly, you're not just selling some random bullshit you came up with, which is what most new business owners do. You're only going to sell something that solves a gigantic problem the niche is already experiencing and is driving them fucking crazy. The motivation to solve this problem is massive and increases your odds of a sale.

Thirdly, you can negotiate your fees on your first three customers if you're new. If they balk at the price, go ahead and drop it, even if you have to drop it a lot. (Just your first three clients though; after that, no price negotiations, you get what you charge and that's that.) Just make sure you get a good testimonial when you're done which will help get future customers.

This won't work because I live in a shithole country where no one has any money.

Incorrect, and you're not listening. This is a *location-independent* business, so it doesn't matter where you live. You can live in the poorest place on Earth, but as long as you have an internet connection (and you know you do), you can sell to people anywhere on the planet. If you live in a lower-tier country, that's great! That means where you live is cheap! Sell to people or companies who live in expensive first-world cities like New York, Vancouver, London, or Tokyo who are accustomed to paying high prices.

Get a small number of clients from these cities, then take these inflated prices they're paying you and live like a little king where you are in your super cheap country. This is called geoarbitrage. It works very well.

I can't hire anyone to do the work for me because they might make a mistake/ piss off my customers/screw up my company.

If you've honestly determined that your Fortress Income is $100,000 per year or less, then it's possible to do this all by yourself or close to it, so having that (largely false) attitude is probably fine. However, if your Fortress Income is more than around $100,000 per year, then that attitude is the wrong one to have. You're going to have to hire people (only virtual assistants or contractors, never employees!) to assist you in running your company, including doing things that are forward-facing (meaning your customers will see what they're doing) to get into the higher income levels. It's mathematically impossible to do it any other way.

Will your staff sometimes make mistakes? Yes. Will your staff sometimes make mistakes on the customers' end? Yup. Do you know what you do when this happens? You apologize, fix it, and move forward, and no one gives a shit. I've had my staff in multiple companies make mistakes both internally and externally, and never once have I lost a customer because of it. Stop being a terrified little bunny rabbit and execute, and you'll find that I'm right.

If you would like me and my team of high-income coaches to take you by the hand and walk you through the process of setting up your own location-independent Alpha 2.0 Business, even if you have no idea how to do it or how to get started, where we guarantee you'll be profitable in 90 days or less, go to 90daybizbuilder.com to join our 90 Day Business Builder program. It's the most popular and successful program I've ever had available to the public, and it will work for you.

Chapter 10

Cashing In On Business Trends In The Collapsing Era

If your business is aligned with a skyrocketing trend, you will make much more money far faster and with less work than if it is not. This is true under normal conditions and it's also true during the era of collapse. Even during collapsing civilizations, there are strong upcoming trends.

In 2009 I started a little internet business showing men how to get dates using online dating. Online dating was a brand new weird little niche back then. Little did I know it was a huge and exploding trend. This little business quickly went to six figures. Just a few years later I was making the same amount of money doing that part-time as I was making as a six-figure business consultant working full-time. I'd love to tell you it's because I'm an amazing businessman, and I'm pretty good, but it's also because I tapped into a sharply growing trend.

When determining the niche for your Alpha 2.0 business, I strongly recommend you find a niche buried inside one of the big growing trends for the 2020s and 2030s. You don't *have* to do this, but I think it's silly not to. If you're going to spend the next several years working in a business, wouldn't you rather have it aligned with a trend so you make way more money than have it be in some stagnating or declining sector?

Listed below are the top business and personal trends over the next ten years or so. Unsurprisingly, most of them are directly related to Western collapse or the AI Black Hole of Unknown. Hey, if the West is collapsing, you might as well make money on it rather than screaming and ranting about it. I make a high income from a business that directly relates to Western collapse (helping people get location-independent and move out of the West) so I can tell you for a fact that many of us are making a lot of money during the collapse and will continue to do so.

Fastest Growing Industries

1. AI

   Of course. The AI Black Hole of Unknown must be fed to grow, so this is the fastest business trend right now. *"But I don't know anything about AI!"* Fine, you don't have to. Find a niche within AI that has some kind of problem that you (or someone you can hire) *can* fix. You don't need to know anything about AI to work within an AI niche.

2. Healthcare

   This is my favorite. Healthcare will absolutely explode all over the world over the next 25 years as people get fatter, sicker, older, and more stressed out. In addition, the West, with its declining birth rates, is going to have hundreds of millions of new old people very soon, and old people need healthcare! It's a fantastic place to find your niche and make a lot of money.

3. E-commerce and Online Retail

   Another obvious one. Just make sure you don't sell low-margin stuff. Instead, as above, sell services or consulting to e-commerce retailers.

4. Renewable Energy

   There is a massive demand for this all over the planet and this will continue to skyrocket for a long time. As someone who lives in the Middle East, I can tell you for a fact that the entire Middle Eastern region (at least the smart countries here) is currently spending trillions of dollars adjusting to a post-oil future.

5. Cybersecurity

   Another one of my favorites. It's hard *not* to make money here.

6. FinTech

   This is a fancy term for moving or storing money digitally. It encompasses a wide range of applications, including digital payments, mobile banking, investment platforms, cryptocurrencies, peer-to-peer lending, and so on.

7. Biotech

   This is driven by two other trends, AI and healthcare. I've made a lot of money here in the past as a business consultant. And again, I knew nothing about biotech; I just helped biotech firms solve problems that they had that I *could* help them with.

8. Pet Care
   This one is hilarious. Far more people own pets now than ever before and this will continue to skyrocket. There was also a surge right after the pandemic. People are so stressed out that dogs and cats provide much-needed emotional support. It's a great trend to cash in on.

9. Smart Appliance Manufacturing
   This one isn't one of my favorites because I believe it's directly tied to consumers spending more money based on debt, but it is technically a growing trend.

10. Sustainable Focus Construction
    This is construction with a focus on sustainable building practices and renewable energy projects. It is very segment-specific so be sure your niche is inside a growing area.

Skyrocketing Business Trends Over The Next Ten Years

Instead of industries, these are the fastest-growing business *trends* that cut across all industries. These trends are listed in order of how fast they are growing.

1. Sustainability and Eco-Friendly Practices
   This tree-hugger stuff is booming and will continue to do so as the Western world continues to shift to the political left. Using recycled materials, reducing carbon footprints, and so on, companies all over the world are going crazy with this stuff. Whether or not you believe in it politically isn't relevant. The point is that it's a strong trend with billions of dollars to be made by people like you.

2. Remote Work and Hybrid Offices
   This was already a trend but the pandemic (the worldwide overreaction to a flu with a 1% death rate) put this on steroids.

3. Digital Transformation and Automation
   Companies are getting more automated and digital to streamline operations and improve customer experiences.

4. Customer Data Analytics and Personalization
   Utilizing "big data" for personalized marketing strategies is becoming crucial as businesses strive to enhance customer engagement and loyalty. I'm doing a lot of this myself these days.

5. Health and Wellness
   This is another post-pandemic trend that shocked a lot of people into focusing on their health a little more. There's also a lot of anti-aging stuff in there for aging Boomers and Gen Xers (like me!).

6. Augmented Reality (AR) and Virtual Reality (VR)
   AR and VR technologies are gaining traction (finally) across various sectors, including retail, education, and training.

Skyrocketing Personal Trends Over The Next Ten Years

Here now are the top *personal* trends for the next 10 years. These are trends people are engaging in instead of companies.

1. Sustainable Living
   More left-winging; things like reducing waste, choosing eco-friendly products, adopting plant-based diets to minimize environmental impact, and all of that stuff.

2. Digital Detox
   People are finally learning to disconnect from technology periodically. A good trend.

3. Personalized Experiences
   Now that companies can provide this, consumers are gravitating more towards tailored experiences in shopping, travel, and entertainment, driven by advancements in data analytics and AI.

4. Financial Literacy and Independence
   As the economics of the West continue to worsen, people have an increasing focus on understanding personal finance, investing, and building wealth through education and smart financial decisions.

5. Community Engagement
   As a reaction to the digital age, many people are now hungry for more real human contact, becoming more involved in their local communities through volunteering, supporting local businesses, and so on. Also, people (and Americans in particular) are far more political now so they tend to participate in social causes more.

6. Lifelong Learning

   I've cashed in on this trend big time. Online courses, workshops, coaching programs, and certifications are all very popular and will continue to be so, especially if niched.

7. Diversity and Inclusion Awareness

   More left-wing stuff again. Social justice issues, diversity, inclusion, DEI, and all that stuff is a strong and growing trend that won't stop (even if people like Trump keep getting elected).

8. Mindfulness and Mental Health Awareness

   Remember the horrible mental health stats I showed you back in Chapter 8? People are trying to maintain or regain their sanity in this collapsing era through things like retreats, meditation, and therapy.

Let me repeat that you don't need to know the technical how-to of any of these industries, niches, or trends to start a business in them. You don't need to know any dentistry to show dentists how to get more clients, for example.

Chapter 11

Doing Business Internationally

Having a location-independent business means you can get clients/customers and thus money from anywhere on the planet instead of just your current town or collapsing Western country. In this chapter, I'm going to give you some ideas and techniques you can use to do this if you wish.

There is no requirement for an Alpha 2.0 Business or your Fortress to sell to people in distant lands. You can indeed be an American and sell to Americans for example; there's nothing wrong with that as long as you follow a few parameters I'll discuss in a minute *and* you build your Fortress. I'm just saying that there are lots of easy ways to make very good money if you broaden your horizons a little and start looking at *the world* as your potential market instead of just your current or favorite country.

If you think this conflicts with my advice about niching, it doesn't. You can be from the UK and find a little narrow niche in Vietnam or Saudi Arabia and make millions. You can also further reduce your taxes and benefit from economic hot spots all over the world in ways you can't with your current or favorite country.

Geoarbitrage

Geoarbitrage is the practice of taking advantage of the cost differences between different countries to make a lot of money. There are many examples of this.

The easiest one is one I've mentioned previously; live in a very cheap country and sell to people who live in very expensive countries or cities. Move to somewhere like Cambodia, the Philippines, or Paraguay which costs a tiny fraction of any collapsing Western country, then have your Alpha 2.0 Business service people or companies in ultra-expensive cities like New York, London, Tokyo, San Francisco, or Paris. It's a genius move. You will live like a king with just a tiny number of clients. I know people who do this and work around 10-15 hours a week while making big incomes.

Here's a more specific example. I'm not sure if this is the case today, but years ago every time Apple would release a new iPhone or iPad, it would come out in the USA first and hit most other countries 3-4 months later. I once worked with a guy who would pay college students in the USA to stand in line at the Apple Store every time a new iPad or iPhone came out (so basically twice a year) to buy the newest thing. He'd get piles of new iPhones and then ship them in huge boxes next-day air to countries in Asia and Oceania where Apple wasn't selling the latest iPhone or iPad yet. He would easily 5X his money every time he did this, getting a huge mountain of cash every six months for very little work.

Value Maxing

You know how some Western men will go to non-Western poor countries to find girlfriends? And how it's often easier for them because as Westerners they are of higher value to women in these lower-end nations than they are with women back at home? Well, international business often works the same way. There are many cases of Americans and British people who were losers in their home countries who went to Japan and almost instantly became famous (in Japan only) because of the fact they were Westerners. Australians consider Americans as much more business-savvy and valuable than other Australians in many cases. Russians often have lots of trouble doing business in non-Russian countries because of the stigma of corruption, causing them to get Western partners who make a decent amount of money just by being a frontman. Westerners who start companies in Africa can often meet with the president of the country within a year or less.

There are so many examples of this you can take advantage of as a Westerner doing business outside of the West.

Sending and Receiving Money

Obviously, you'll need something like PayPal and/or Stripe to receive payments from your clients, but on the international stage, you'll want many more options than that. You want to set up several other ways to pay and get paid, including:

- Cryptocurrency, especially Bitcoin, Ethereum, USDC, and Tether USDT
- International money transfer/cross-border payment platforms, like Wise and/or Revolut, but Payoneer is also good and there are several others.
- The ability to send international wire transfers from your bank whenever you need to without having to call your bank on the phone.

Here's the bottom line: the more ways you have to receive money and send money, the more money you will make, all other factors being equal. So don't limit yourself to just PayPal and your collapsing domestic Western bank.

Caleb's 40% Rule

I've heard this objection once or twice: *"Hey Caleb, if you move out of the USA and internationalize, then when the USA collapses, you'll still be screwed because all of your customers are still in the USA! So you did all that stuff for nothing!"*

This person usually thinks they're some kind of genius as if that thought had never occurred to me. When, in fact, it did, over 15 years ago when I started on this journey. This is when I initiated what I call my 40% Rule. It's not a requirement for your Fortress. It's simply something I'm doing personally as a precaution; feel free to do it yourself, or not, or do some kind of variant.

My 40% Rule means that of all the income from all of my businesses, income streams, and investments, I only want a maximum of 40% to come from the Collapsing Trifecta. In other words, if I look at the past 12 months of my total income from all of my businesses and investments, I want the United States, Canada, and all the nations in Europe to only represent 40% of that figure at the most. The other 60% must come from non-Western countries (though Australia and New Zealand are also allowed since they're Western and in very big trouble but I don't think they're going to full-on collapse, as I explained back in Chapter 2).

This way, when these countries finally go down the toilet, I'll lose a maximum of around 40% of my income, which isn't great, but it's tolerable because I've already built my Fortress, with my Fortress Income, Fortress Taxes, Fortress Net Worth, and Fortress Cash.

Compare that to normal Westerners who will lose 100% of their incomes when the West collapses and they have no net worth or savings at all.

The way I've responded to those making these kinds of objections in the past is that I say that when the USA (or Canada or Europe) collapses, I will be *inconvenienced,* while you will be *fucked.* I'd much rather be inconvenienced than completely fucked, thank you very much. Making the argument that you'd rather be completely fucked than putting in the work to be just inconvenienced instead doesn't make any sense.

As of this writing, my 40% Rule is still a goal I'm working toward, since there are indeed still times when my Collapsing Trifecta income is indeed over 40% of my total. I'm still working on it and it improves every year. In the long term, I'd like to have the vast majority of my income come from high-growth regions in Asia (especially China, India, Vietnam, and Cambodia) and the Middle East (especially Saudi Arabia, UAE, Bahrain, and Qatar) as well as some regions of Latin America (particularly Colombia and Paraguay) and I make strong inroads into these places all the time, all because of my 40% Rule.

Do You Need To Learn Another Language?

This question comes up a lot. If you decide to move to or do business in South America, do you need to learn Spanish? If you're going to move to or do business in Eastern Europe, should you learn Russian? What about learning Chinese? Arabic? Something else?

Here's the short answer: Learning the language of the region you've chosen *will* strongly help you, both in your personal life and your ability to make money. No question about that. But you don't absolutely *need* to do it.

When I say this, some people get offended and say how dare you, if you move to a Spanish-speaking country you need to shut the hell up, have some decency, respect the locals, and learn Spanish. Uh, actually, no you don't. I live almost half of my life in Paraguay where virtually no one speaks any English, and I get along just fine. I'm here right now as I type these words. I've done business here, conducted financial transactions here, and even dated women here without speaking any Spanish other than a few basic phrases.

I've done the same thing all over the world where I didn't speak the local language. Modern-day technology (i.e. the Google Translate app on your phone) more than makes up for the fact that I don't speak the language. In less than three years from now, you'll likely have an AI earpiece you can wear that will translate any language you hear into English in real-time, and everyone else will also be wearing it so you won't need to speak their language either.

I admit that using a language translation app can be a little inconvenient at times, but it works, and no one cares or gets offended.

Again I will repeat, learning the language of your chosen flag *does* help, a lot. If you want to do it, please do it. But don't feel like you need to, because you don't.

Part 4

How To Internationalize For Maximum Freedom and Defense

Chapter 12

Five Flags

Back in Chapter 7, I laid out the six levels of internationalizing your life. The final level, level 6, is Five Flags. Five Flags is the strongest way to minimize your taxes, maximize your freedom and personal sovereignty, maximize your long-term safety and security, and maximize your travel mobility all at the same time. Setting up Five Flags in your life is the best way to build your Fortress. It essentially turns your Fortress from a castle made of stone to one made of steel.

The Requirements For Five Flags

Despite its numerous amazing advantages, doing the full Five Flags setup is complicated and expensive, and requires time, travel, effort, patience, and money to establish and maintain. Also, doing the *entire* Five Flags system has several requirements first:

- 100% location-independent income. If your income is location-dependent, Five Flags isn't possible.
- Your own business or businesses. Five Flags doesn't work for employees, even remote ones.
- A decently high income, at least around $180,000 USD per year. Otherwise, the costs and effort involved might not be worth the tax benefits.
- A willingness to travel internationally a lot, at least for 12-18 months, while you set everything up.
- A high level of patience and emotional control. In the initial stages, you'll be dealing with a lot of government bureaucrats, paperwork, lawyers, and accountants, all of whom can be a big pain in the ass.
- Several advisors/experts who can help you through the process. You will not be able to do all of this yourself. (We can help you at calebjones.com.)

Thus, doing the full Five Flags setup is purely optional. If you're not at the above level yet, you can implement *parts* of Five Flags without doing all of it, or you can set Five Flags as a goal and work towards it, as I did many years ago.

If you do meet all of the requirements above, then in my opinion, Five Flags *should* be something you implement immediately. It will transform your entire life into something far better. By the end of this chapter, you'll see why.

How 5 Flags Works

The Five Flags structure is a portfolio of five or more "flags." A "flag" in this context means a country you designate to serve a particular purpose. Speaking in general, there are several different types of flags, including but not limited to:

- Living Flag – A country where you spend a lot of months every year (you can even have more than one).
- Passport Flag – A country where you have their passport (i.e. citizenship) but don't live there.
- Residency Flag – A country where you have residency but don't live.
- Backup Flag – The country that is your international backup plan (as I talked about in Chapter 7)
- Economic Flag – A country where you have a corporation or investments.
- Dating Flag – A country where you don't live full time but where you go often to date people or see long-distance lovers.
- Recreational Flag – A country you don't live in but visit often for fun or vacations.

You can have one or more of these flags. For example, you can have one Living Flag, two Passport Flags (meaning you have two passports), a Backup Flag, and two Recreational Flags. You can design any system you want.

Five Flags is a specific structure of five of these flags arrayed in a particular way. I call these your Countries A, B, C, D, and E.

Your Country A – Where You Live

This is a Living Flag where you live half or most of the year but where you are *not* a citizen, do *not* have a passport there, and have *no assets there* other than perhaps a day-to-day bank account for groceries and other basics.

You do this for three reasons:

1. The government of Country A either can't or is less likely to tax you, because you're not a citizen there, only an expat resident. Every country is different regarding specific tax laws, but across the board, a country

is far less likely to tax you or give a shit about your income if you're not a citizen there. This means that your Country A must be a country that does *not* tax your worldwide income even if you stay there for more than six months at a time. There are approximately 30 countries in the world like this.

2. The government of Country A can't ever confiscate your stuff because you have no assets there. Any assets you have are in other countries far away where your Country A has no power. I'm reminded of John McAfee, who wisely moved from the Collapsing USA to Belize. The problem is that he moved all of his assets and money there too. Then he proceeded to buy land and houses in his new Living Flag (more assets). Everything was great until the government of Belize came in one day and seized every asset he owned. He barely escaped the country, lost everything, and had to start all over financially while in his sixties. Not smart. Had he followed Five Flags by not moving any assets there, not buying any there, and just renting his house, he would have lost nothing.

3. You are always subject to far fewer laws in a country if you're a non-citizen than if you are a full citizen. This means more freedom for you if you don't have citizenship in your Country A where you live (legal *residency* is okay, and needed, just not *citizenship*). As just one example, in my Country A, Dubai in the UAE, if I were a citizen of the UAE (which I am not and don't want to be) I would have been *forced by law* to take the COVID-19 vaccine during the pandemic. But because I'm a non-citizen resident, none of those laws apply to me, so I'm not vaccinated and the UAE government doesn't care.

Your Country B – Where You Have Citizenship

Your Country B is the opposite of your Country A. Country B is the country (or countries because you can have more than one of these flags) where you have full citizenship and a valid passport but where you *don't live*. You don't even spend a lot of time there, other than brief visits to do things like visit your family and pick up a few things you like that are only available there (if any).

Since you don't live there, your Country B isn't going to tax you. However, you can still use their passport for things like traveling, getting visa-free access to certain countries, opening bank accounts, and so on. It's the best of both worlds. The one partial exception is, as always, the Collapsing USA which will still tax you on any income you make past about $130,000 a year (and going higher every year), but even then there are many ways to reduce taxes further if you don't live in the USA and limit your time there. So having the USA as your Country B is still acceptable, though in my opinion if that's your only passport you should actively work on getting some more.

Regardless of which nation is your Country B, ideally, you need at least two passports. This way if there is ever a serious problem with one of these countries (they go to war, they collapse, they pass a bunch of unfavorable tax laws, they become more authoritarian, etc), you've got a second passport as a backup.

There are several ways to get a second passport, but some are illegal and others are only available to the elites. For normal people who want to follow the law, there are three methods you can use to get a second passport:

1. You can buy it for a low six-figure amount. This is called "citizen by investment" and many Caribbean countries offer passports like this. This is the most expensive way to get a second passport but it's also the fastest by far (it only takes 4-6 months instead of several years) and it's 100% guaranteed.
2. If you have ancestry in a country, meaning you have parents, grandparents, or great-grandparents who were born there, you can possibly get your citizenship that way. This is an extremely paperwork-intensive method and will take about 2-3 years plus a lot of legal work, but it does work.
3. You can make the country your temporary Country A and de facto live there, spending most of the year there for several years. After 3-15 years (and every country mandates a different number of years and months per year you need to be there), you can then apply for citizenship. This is the cheapest way to get a second passport but it takes the longest by far.

To be clear, you don't *need* multiple passports to make Five Flags work or to have a valid Country B. In most cases, you can just have Country B be your ex-home country. It's just that multiple passports are strongly recommended.

Your Country C – Where Your Business Is Located

Your Country C is where you base your legal business entity (corporation, LLC, or similar) and at least one business checking account in that country attached to that corporation. You need to make sure you use a country with zero or low corporate taxes and that is at least somewhat friendly to foreign business owners. This gives you several advantages:

1. You pay minimal or zero corporate taxes.
2. Where you live (Country A) and where you're a citizen (Country B) has no power or authority over your business, protecting you from any governments, problems, tax laws, bail-ins, or lawsuits in those countries.
3. Your Countries A and B (usually) have no idea that business is there, adding to your privacy and asset protection. (Exception: Americans usually have to report it to the US government. Of course, right?)

Just like it's a good idea to have two passports, ideally, at least in the long-term, you should have two Countries C. Banks are finicky things in the era of the Creeping Darkness, so if you have your "main" Country C and a "backup" Country C, then if you ever have a problem with your bank or government in your main Country C, you just shift to your other country and have no disruption in income.

You never keep a lot of cash in your Country C's bank accounts. Holding long-term assets would be for your County D…

Your Country D – Where Your Assets Are Located

Your Country D (and you can have many Countries D) is the country or countries where you store your long-term assets and investments. You don't want your assets in your Country A where you live and where they can be taken, nor in your Country B where the government there can tax them and/or confiscate them. You also don't want them sitting in a bank in your Country C because banks aren't good places for long-term asset holding. No, you want your assets in other countries where you don't live, don't have citizenship, and ideally, don't do business.

By "assets" I mean anything that can be a long-term investment, including stocks, bonds, commodities, precious metals, real estate, and so on. For your key assets, you need to make sure your Country D is stable and respects property rights. You also need to ensure they don't tax any capital gains for non-residents (and most countries don't).

For more risky or speculative investments, you can choose any country you think will do well. If any laws in your Country A or B require you to report these assets to them, you do so you do to be legally compliant (then start looking for new Countries A and B, because fuck them). The good news is that most countries don't care, and the few that do (like the Collapsing USA, as usual) often have at least some exceptions to certain assets you don't need to report.

Now you can have protected assets that few (or no one) know about on which you never need to pay any capital gains taxes.

If you have lots of assets, you want lots of Country Ds, not just one. Always diversify. Unless you have very few assets, don't throw all of your assets into one Country D no matter how much you like it. That's not sound financial management, especially not with the Creeping Darkness at our doorsteps.

Your Country E – Where You Vacation And Buy Your Stuff

Your Country E, which I consider optional, is a country (or countries) that has zero sales tax and zero VAT taxes on foreigners and has extremely low prices on certain things you purchase often. You use this country as a vacation spot and/or where you buy your stuff, using our friend geoarbitrage once again to save a lot of money.

There are many examples of this. Buying electronics or computers in Singapore is shockingly cheaper than buying them anywhere in the Collapsing West. You can vacation to beaches in the Philippines to locations that are more beautiful than anything in Hawaii at one-tenth the price. Auto or motorcycle enthusiasts save thousands of dollars buying their auto parts in Japan than anywhere in the USA or Canada. If you're going to buy your girlfriend or wife a nice diamond ring, you're going to spend far less on jewelry like that in India, Thailand, or Dubai than anywhere in the Collapsing West.

The opportunities for your Country E are endless and really depend on you, the region of the world you live in, what you like, and your lifestyle. You'll save thousands upon thousands of dollars a year on stuff you'd purchase anyway.

The Elements Required for Five Flags

Here's the summary list of what you need in place for Five Flags to be fully set up.

- Legal residency in at least one country not including where you have your passport. This would be your Country A. Additional residencies are optional. (I have permanent, legal residency in five different countries.)
- A corporation and bank account in another country, your Country C. Sometimes residency is required in your Country C because many

countries require residency before you can set up corporations or bank accounts there. Having residency in your Country C is not a violation of Five Flags.

- Investment accounts, and/or foreign real estate in your Country D. Residency is usually not required for these things but they can be.
- A corporate structure that minimizes your taxes based on your Five Flags setup. This can sometimes mean that one of your corporations owns another one of your corporations or LLCs. We'll talk more about specific international corporate structures in Chapter 16.

This also means that you have traveled around a bit and have identified:

- Where you want to live (Country A) since everyone will have different tastes. We'll talk about how to find the best country for you in Chapter 14.
- What the best country is to start a business based on your personal citizenship, tax burden, and preferences (Country C).
- Where to store your assets, if you have any (Country D), since there are many options.

We'll discuss most of these things later in this book.

What Five Flags Gives You

Once you set up your Five Flags structure, you are, quite literally, one of the freest, most protected, most mobile, most private, and lowest-taxed human beings on the planet, more so than even most celebrities or billionaires. The advantages and benefits to you are so numerous that I couldn't list them all here, but here are just a few of the more obvious ones.

- Your total taxes drop to below 5%, and in many cases 1% or even 0% even if you make a six-, seven-, or eight-figure income. And this is all 100% legal. It's a nice way to achieve your Fortress Taxes (15% or less)
- Supreme asset protection. Your assets are far more protected than they ever could be before. The odds of ever losing them to any government, ex-wife, or lawsuit drop to almost zero.
- Your mobility is massive; you can travel to pretty much any country in the world you want, usually without ever having to mess around with any visas. During times of war, pandemic, or collapse, you're still mobile because any country where you have legal residency or citizenship has to let you in.

- Massive savings in your cost of living.
- Massive diversification options in terms of banks, investments, and international currencies previously unavailable.
- No individual country in the world can cause you any major problems, ever, for the rest of your life. If any one of your flags goes bad, you just pivot to one of your others, and you continue on your merry way. No one country, government, or group of stupid voters can ever cause major problems for you. Every time you hear news about how a particular country's taxes are going up, or they just elected a horrible new president or prime minister, or is increasing more socialist or authoritarian laws, or is going to war, or has bank failures or stock market crashes, or is suffering a horrible recession or depression, or is cracking down on cryptocurrency, or a new pandemic breaks out, or whatever, while everyone else is freaking out, you barely give a shit and your happy life continues (and if any of this stuff happens in your Country A where you live, you just leave).

In addition, Five Flags covers a lot of ground in terms of building your Fortress:

- It establishes your non-Western base.
- It establishes your Fortress Taxes.
- It protects both your Fortress Cash *and* Fortress Net Worth.

Five Flags is awesome. Regardless, as you can see, there are a lot of moving parts to Five Flags. If you meet all of the requirements of Five Flags at the beginning of this chapter, I would suggest you start making your Five Flags plan now. It will take possibly as long as 1-3 years to get it all done, so the time to start is right now before the Creeping Darkness hits you.

If you don't meet all the requirements for Five Flags, that's okay. You probably have gleaned some cool ideas for yourself regarding what *pieces* of Five Flags might work for you. At a bare minimum, you need Level 3 of internationalizing, which is an international backup plan to establish your non-Western base for your Fortress, and this does *not* require Five Flags (remember, Five Flags is Level 6). With the information you'll learn in the rest of this book, you'll be able to flesh out your international plan regardless of your current scenario.

Chapter 13

Putting It All Together And Developing Your International Plan

Now that you fully understand all of your options regarding your overall international plan, you can start to put a customized plan together for yourself so you can build your Fortress.

As we discussed back in Chapter 7, there are six levels to internationalization. As a quick review, they are:

Level 1: Offshoring
Level 2: Nomad
Level 3: International Backup Plan
Level 4: Expat
Level 5: Multi-Non-Western Home
Level 6: Five Flags

As I also explained, Levels 1 and 2 aren't going to adequately build your Fortress since it doesn't get you a non-Western base, one of the eight Fortress components. This means you must choose Level 3 or higher. Levels 4 and higher require location-independent income through your Alpha 2.0 Business which means if you don't have location-independent income yet, you'll have to choose Level 3 for now and upgrade yourself to Levels 4 or higher once you have the location-independent income.

With all of these variables, here's a simple system that will show you exactly which level you need. Just go through the following questions below.

Question #1: Do you currently own your own business which represents the majority of your income?
If no: Choose International Backup Plan.
If yes: Go to the next question.

Question #2: Do you currently have 100% location-independent income?
If no: Choose International Backup Plan.
If yes: Go next question.

Question #3: Are you willing to move out of your current Western country within the next 12-18 months?

If no: Choose International Backup Plan.

If yes: Go to the next question.

Question #4: Do you currently make more than about $180,000 USD per year or the equivalent? This means net profit income from your business before you pay taxes.

> If no: Choose International Backup Plan, Expat, or Multi-Non-Western Home
>
> If yes: Choose Five Flags, or at least as much of Five Flags as you're willing to do.

Creating Your International Back-Up Plan

If, based on the above analysis, you're going to choose the International Backup Plan as your option, here's your battle plan on how to get started:

1. Pick your backup country. This decision should be based on your interests, tastes, age, personality, goals, and family situation. This is an important decision so I'll explain exactly how to do that in Chapter 14, but the point is that you need to start researching this now.
2. Set aside at least one week in your schedule to fly to this country and spend at least one week there, either to check it out to see if you like it, or to get residency there if you've already been there and know you love it. I'll talk more about this in Chapter 14, but the point here is to schedule that time now. If you have your own business, figure this out with your schedule, team, and clients. If you have a job, make whatever arrangements with your boss you need to make to take the time off to do this. If this makes you nervous, remember weekends. You can take five days off work for a nine-day vacation if you add in both adjacent weekends. You can also make arrangements with your boss (if you have a job) or clients/team (if you have a business) to do remote work while you're there, since this isn't technically a "vacation," this is a research trip, so doing work on this trip is allowed.
3. Once you've determined you like the country and want it as your backup plan, you need to get legal residency there, which will require a trip there for 7-30 days depending on the country. You can use our services at calebjones.com (we offer residency services for our favorite top four or five countries), or hire a legal firm to do it for you, or in

some cases you can do it yourself (which I generally don't recommend, but it's doable with certain countries if you're very patent, have a decent amount of free time, and speak the local language).

4. Once you get residency there, set up a bank account there and deposit some cash in their local currency. Make very sure you get a debit card with the VISA or Mastercard symbol on it that is linked to the bank account. Getting an actual *credit* card is not necessary unless you really want one; the *debit* card is mandatory.

5. Set up some kind of easy system of transferring money from your Western bank account to your backup country's account. International wire transfers usually work fine but services like Wise, Payoneer, or Revolut are often easier and cheaper. If your country is particularly backward with its banks then the worst-case scenario is that you bring a wad of cash down with you (less than $10,000 or else you'll have to declare it) and deposit it that way. Another worst-case scenario is that you can use services like Western Union or MoneyGram to send cash to either yourself or someone in that country you trust (a trusted friend or your attorney there) and they can deposit it for you in your bank.

6. You're going to have to start leaving stuff there so you have all of your living amenities whenever you visit. For example, I like having my favorite chair, a nice fan by my bed when I sleep, my favorite brand of teeth flossers that aren't available in the country, and so on. You can't bring all of this crap there every time you fly to and from the country, so you need some way of keeping it there when you aren't present. You have three options for this:

    a. Leave it all with a close friend or attorney there. This is the cheapest option but not the safest.

    b. Rent a year-round storage unit there and leave it all there whenever you leave. When you come back, just go pick it all up and bring it to your hotel or Airbnb. This will cost you well less than $80 per month in most countries. This is much safer than leaving it with someone and is far less expensive than having a year-round home there. I have storage units in several countries all over the world, including the USA, Mexico, and Hong Kong. I also had storage units in Dubai and Paraguay before I moved to these countries permanently.

c. If it's a cheap country and you can afford it and you want to do it, rent a year-round house or apartment there. This is the most convenient option by far, again if you can afford it. My year-round apartment in Paraguay is only $500 per month and it's in a new building in the nicest neighborhood in the country with all the usual Western amenities. You can also rent out your apartment for the months you aren't there; just make sure one of the rooms or big closets has a lock on it (or install one) and leave your stuff in there when you leave.

Let me tell you something. You will not believe the feeling of happiness, peace, and security you'll have once you set all of this up in your backup country. Once you have all of these things in place, all of the usual problems in your current collapsing Western country will immediately bother you less, because *now you have somewhere to go* if there are any major issues.

It also makes all future trips there have more meaning and excitement for you. Every time you go there, you'll have this feeling of *building something exciting*. You'll meet new long-term contacts, learn more aspects of the culture that you can use in the future, get better at speaking the local language (if they don't already speak English, and many countries do), get more items for your apartment or storage unit to make your life more comfortable, get more clients and/or contacts for your business, and many other things. If you're single, you can date people there and carry on real relationships (albeit possibly ones that are sometimes long-distance, but that's okay under certain conditions). It's just awesome.

Then, of course, at any time you're ready, you can make your backup country your actual living flag and move there full-time (or most of the time) whenever the hell you want, making it a very easy transition. This is exactly how I moved to Dubai. It started as a backup flag for a time. I would spend a few weeks a year there several times a year with my storage unit, and then I just moved there and got an apartment. Same with Paraguay. I had already set up my legal residency in both countries so it was a breeze.

Residency Factors

Now we need to address some of the concerns you might have about moving to another country or setting up your international backup plan.

The first one is residency factors. As I've already explained, any international option above Level 2 will require you to get legal residency in your new flag country. If you're just using visitor's visas to access the country then any time there's a big problem in the world (economic collapse, war, pandemic, etc) that country will likely bar you from entry, but if you have legal residency they have to let you in. This was tested and proven correct during the COVID-19 pandemic (the worldwide overreaction to a flu with a 1% death rate, and no, I'm not going to let that go) when many people were barred entry to countries all over the planet during all of the lockdowns, yet all of these countries let people with residency in with no problems. (The only exception to this I'm aware of was Authoritarian Australia, so you probably shouldn't live there.)

When I say "residency" or "legal residency" this can be *temporary* residency or *permanent* residency. A lot of people are concerned about getting permanent residency and are scared of temporary residency for some reason, but it really doesn't matter because they're both the same damn thing. In most countries, temporary residency means you need to renew your residency in 1-3 years, and "permanent" residency means you need to renew it every 5-8 years or so. Even the touted Golden Visa in the UAE needs to be renewed every 10 years. This means that "permanent" residency *isn't permanent at all*. It's just a longer version of temporary. To be fair, there are some exceptions to this where permanent really does mean permanent (meaning you *never* have to renew the residency), like Mexico, but these countries are the exception, not the rule.

Getting residency means you need to get residency in a country that offers legal residency without you having to move there *unless* you're doing Level 4 or higher and are planning on living there most of the year. If you're not planning on living there most of the year yet, then as of the writing of this book, these are the only countries that offer legal residency without having to live there full-time:

Caribbean
Bahamas
Antigua and Barbuda
St. Kitts and Nevis
Dominica
Grenada
St. Lucia

Europe
Portugal
Spain
Greece
Armenia
Malta
Cyprus
Latvia
Turkey
Montenegro
Asia
Malaysia
Singapore
Thailand
Cambodia
Latin America
Paraguay
Ecuador
Mexico
Costa Rica
Belize
Panama
Other
Vanuatu
United Arab Emirates

To repeat, if you plan on living in your new country for most of the year, the above list is irrelevant and you can go pretty much anywhere you want. But if you're looking for residency for something like an international backup plan, you're going to have to choose from one of the above countries.

The trick is that many of the above countries require a lot of money to be invested or verified for you to get residency, often $50K to $200K or more. If you don't have a lot of money (yet) then these won't be an option for you.

My personal favorite short list of easy, don't-need-to-live-there residency countries that don't require a lot of investment or extreme financial verification are the UAE, Paraguay, Armenia, and Mexico. A few more, which I don't like quite as much but are still good living flags or backup flags, are Panama, Cambodia, Costa Rica, and several others.

The last factor you need to verify is to make sure that your new country will allow residents from your country. For example, if you want residency in Armenia but your passport is from Azerbaijan, you might have a problem. There are also a few countries that don't want to take in residents from certain African countries as well. Just do the research and verify that your current country is okay with your new country before you spend a lot of time on it; it's usually not a problem.

Family Factors

"But what about my family???" you ask.

In Chapter 15 I'm going to address this objection/fear in detail. Just because your stubborn dad or asshole little brother doesn't want to leave the country doesn't mean you need to stay there to go down with the ship, but I'll address that soon.

That being said, there are isolated and rare scenarios where your family situation *might* affect your decision regarding internationalizing.

One possible scenario is that you have small children and you are no longer in a relationship with the other parent, meaning he/she has at least 50% custody of your kids. Ideally, you could convince the other parent to move to your new country with you and bring your kid(s), but this is often unlikely. This means your kids are going to stay in your collapsing Western country, creating a difficult decision for you.

To be clear, this scenario only applies if you have *small* children, "small" in this case means under the age of 16. If all of your kids are over the age of about 15, they're going to do whatever they want, and now they fall into that "adults can make their own decisions" category that I will describe in Chapter 15. Staying in your collapsing country and going down with the ship just because your stubborn, left-wing, Gen Z, 23-year-old daughter doesn't want to leave is, once again, a stupid and irrational decision on your part. Move out of your collapsing country and visit your daughter two or three times a year. It's not a big deal. My daughter is 26 and my son is 33, and this is exactly what I do. My son has already left the Collapsing USA years ago. He does the Multi-Non-Western Home option and splits his time between Mexico and Thailand. My daughter still lives in the USA at the moment but eventually wants to move to Italy or Argentina. I see my kids at least twice a year, sometimes more.

If your kids are indeed still little and you have no legal authority to take them with you because your ex isn't cooperating, then yes, this does make things a little complicated, but it's still not a showstopper. You still have several options, including:

1. You could just leave the country anyway and visit your kids as much as you can.
2. You can stay in your current country but set up your International Backup Plan, then quickly and easily move to your new country as soon as your youngest child turns 16 or so.
3. You could live in your new country for X number of months a year and be back in your current Western country for the rest of the year. You may even be able to take your kids with you to your new country for extended but temporary visits, especially during the summer when school is out.

Don't be like most people when it comes to these international strategies and just throw your arms in the air in surrender just because you have small kids and aren't with the other parent. You're just being one of those seatbelt people who are looking for excuses to do nothing. You still have lots of options, you can still make it work, and I personally know many people who have done so even though they still have small kids with their exes.

The next possible but unlikely scenario is that you have one or two family members who require constant medical or logistical care, like an aging or disabled parent. Like with the small kids example, these scenarios are not the showstoppers you think they are. The main thing is that in most cases, these people can come with you. And because they're old or disabled, they really don't have a choice in the matter. "Mom, I'm going to continue to take care of you, but we're moving to Costa Rica next summer and you're coming with me," and that's that.

Let's be honest here; "aging" or "disabled" does not mean this person can't get on an airplane for a single nine-hour flight one time. This person *can* move out of the Collapsing West with you. They may not *want* to go, they may complain loudly about it, but they *can*, and you know it. It's the same scenario as when you have to restrict an aging parent who can't safely drive anymore from driving cars. They will scream at you and call you all kinds of names when you take their keys away and tell them they can no longer drive a car, but regardless you know it's the right thing to do for them. Getting them out of the Collapsing West is *the exact same thing*. You making excuses about this is just hurting *them*.

There is a rare and remote possibility that this aging/disabled person requires highly specialized, regular medical care that you *think* is unavailable in your new country, and now you have a new excuse. The key word in that sentence is that you *think* it's not available. Do the research; you might be surprised. Countries like Panama, Singapore, UAE, and Malaysia, just to name a few, have *superior* medical care and facilities than most collapsing Western countries including the United States, and often this care is less expensive. Also, some or all of this care can be administered remotely, meaning your relative can be anywhere in the world and still receive it.

This is a perfect segue for the next factor…

Medical Factors

The next factor you may have to consider, and another common excuse for doing nothing, is medical issues. You might be concerned that you (or a loved one) have unique medical needs that might be disrupted if you leave your collapsing Western country. Working with hundreds of people over the past ten years or so, plus my own experiences with this has clearly shown me that this is seldom a showstopper problem.

I'll give you a common example: me. I'm on testosterone replacement therapy (TRT), meaning I take testosterone and other injections that I administer myself several times a week. I will do this for the rest of my life (until and unless the AI overloads invent another option). Most of these injections are available by prescription only in most parts of the world, and I need to have these pharmaceuticals at all times. In addition, I also take several odd vitamins and medications for my anti-aging protocols because I want to look and feel as young as I can as I get older. Sometimes these things aren't available in all countries.

So here's what I *didn't* do. I didn't throw my arms up in surrender and say, "Oh well, because I need these pharmaceuticals I guess I'm stuck in the Collapsing USA for the rest of my life and I'll just be fucked when it collapses!" No, instead I did the research, spoke with doctors and pharmacists in other countries, and spoke with other international men who are on similar protocols and asked what they do.

I found that much of what I need is indeed available in other countries outside of the USA. Indeed, in many non-Western countries, medications that are prescription-only are over-the-counter instead, making this even easier. I've seen several diabetics complain that they can't leave the collapsing West and move to Latin America because they need insulin when insulin is a very inexpensive, over-the-counter drug in most Latin countries that is easily obtainable!

The few items I need that I can't get (or can't easily get) outside of the USA I either have shipped to me internationally or if that's not an option (and sometimes it isn't), I just pick up a six or twelve-month supply whenever I visit the USA for other reasons (usually business or to visit my extended family). Once I got a system down, I have literally never had a problem with this.

You can do the same thing. It's extremely rare for someone to have a medical condition where the above model won't work.

In addition, you can conduct your doctor appointments remotely (over video conferencing, texting, and email) and even get blood work done in your new country and just email your doctor the results back in your Western country.

If you need some kind of major one-time surgery, fine, schedule your surgery for when you need it, go back to your Western country (if you have to, and often you don't need to), have your surgery, recover, and then go back home to your new country. *This shit is not complicated. You're just making it complicated because you're scared and/or lazy and making excuses.*

I'm going to repeat that a huge number of non-Western countries have *superior* and *less expensive* healthcare than the Collapsing West. Canadian and European healthcare is a fucking mess, and the healthcare in the USA is an absolute rip-off. You can often find the exact same pills made at the exact same facility that cost $120 a bottle in the USA but $8 a bottle in Mexico.

When I got COVID-19 while living in Dubai, I went to the doctor at a high-tech medical facility, had a comprehensive check-up, the doctor *gave me his personal phone number* and checked up on me several times over the next few days. Total cost to me, including all prescriptions: $220 USD. This would have been over $1,000 in the USA.

I was once sick in Paraguay and I went to a private hospital there. They gave me several different IV drips, prescribed some pills, and fixed me right up ASAP, literally making me feel better the next day. Total cost to me, including prescriptions: less than $60 USD.

I've had numerous visits to doctors and hospitals all over the world in my non-Western flags and I've never been disappointed and always saved a shitload of money.

Financial Factors

Your Western VISA or Mastercard credit cards and debit cards will work in just about every country in the world with very rare exceptions. Some banks might charge you a 1% international transaction fee or something like that, but many banks don't. (Ask your bank if you're not sure.) You can put your Western debit card into any ATM in just about any country in the world and immediately withdraw cash in their local currency.

This isn't the 1960s when you had to worry about carrying around a wad of local currency or traveler's checks to buy things in a distant land. You can just go to just about any country you want with zero cash of any kind and your debit and credit cards will work just fine.

That being said, to adhere to Fortress Model parameters, you will need a local bank account in local currency, at least for your backup flag. This is not only for backup and protection reasons, but it's also so you can send money to anyone or any company inside that country without having to screw around with international wires or things like that. Your grocery store will take your credit/debit card, but the guy who installs your bookshelf probably won't, so you'll need to either give him cash (which is a pain in the ass) or do a local bank transfer with your local bank's app (which is easy and painless).

This is why I said you need a system of regularly sending money from your Western bank account to your new non-Western one, at least until you convert your entire finances over to non-Western currencies, which is a very good idea and a goal to strive for, but might take more time (and is not technically required for your Fortress).

Lastly and perhaps most importantly, you need to work with a good accountant or tax attorney in your former Western country to determine taxes once you leave. If you're just doing an International Backup Plan and staying in your current Western country then this isn't necessary yet. But if you are actually leaving, you need to determine exactly how you can move your tax status from your Western country to your new living flag, as well as determine if there are any exit taxes or final capital gains taxes due when you make your move. Once this is done, congratulations, you don't have to pay huge and ridiculous Western taxes anymore, for the rest of your life…

…unless you're an American. Sigh. As always, the Collapsing USA is an exception, so even if you leave the USA and never return they will require you at the point of gun to file annual tax returns for the rest of your life and if your income is high, you'll possibly have to keep paying them at least some taxes as well. If you don't do this, they may cancel your passport and arrest you at the airport as soon as you return. It sure is a good thing the USA is a "free country" and the "Land of the Free" and the "freest country in the world."

If you are an American you need to take advantage of the Foreign Earned Income Exclusion or FEIE. If you stay out of the USA for most of the year and adhere to certain requirements, the first $130,000 (or so) you make annually will be tax-free (but you still have to file a tax return). The bad news is that if you make more than this, you will pay some American taxes, even if you never go back to the USA. The only way around this is to renounce your American citizenship, which is a big, scary step that most Americans won't take. The good news is that the $130,000 figure goes up every year as it adjusts for inflation.

Relationship Factors

If you are married to or live with a significant other, obviously this person should go with you and be all in on your international plans. You need to involve this person in selecting a new country for both of you so that you have some buy-in on his or her end. Everything like residency, bank accounts, and so on need to apply to this person just like they apply to you. The good news is that getting secondary residencies for things like spouses, girlfriends, and minor children is usually pretty easy.

If you have kids, then obviously you need to look at schools in your new flags and use that as one of your deciding factors. As usual, you will be absolutely shocked at the high quality of schools outside of the Collapsing West.

If you are more or less single then you can date in your new country, and indeed this is one of the biggest reasons why men leave the Collapsing West; easier dating opportunities with more attractive women. Hey, whatever gets you out of the Collapsing West is fine with me. Just make sure that your new country has the type of women you like. We'll discuss that more in the next chapter.

Chapter 14

How To Pick The Best Country For You

There are approximately 195 countries on planet Earth. All this talk about setting up a backup plan or moving to another country is nice, but what if you have absolutely no idea where to get started or what kind of country you would like?

No problem. I'm about to show you how to find the exact country (or countries) for you. It's a decision that will require some thought and research, but it's not nearly as complicated as you think.

The most important thing to realize is that you must choose a country based on what *you* want. And I mean *you*. Don't make the common internet mistake of choosing a country that your best friend likes, or that your favorite internet guru likes (including me), or that you heard on a forum was good, or that you read about in a favorable article, or saw in a cool YouTube video. These people aren't you. You're you. You have a unique set of parameters that are going to apply to you and you alone.

Here are a few examples of what I mean.

If you're an extrovert, you probably want a country that is exciting and has a vibrant social scene and nightlife. If you're an introvert, you probably don't care about any of that, can move to a super boring country, and be perfectly happy there. The same goes for (possibly) if you're young (you want more fun stuff to do) or if you're much older (you just want to relax in a quiet environment).

If you're single, you probably want a place with a fantastic dating scene with friendly, easy, good-looking women (or men if you're a woman). If you're married or otherwise committed, you probably don't care about that very much.

If you have very little money, you probably want a place that is super cheap to live. If you make a lot of money, the cost of living probably doesn't matter much to you, and you probably want a place that is really nice with lots of first-world amenities.

Some people like colder weather, other people like warmer weather. Some people really need to be near the ocean, while other people don't give a shit. Some people can tolerate humidity, other people can't stand even a little bit of it. Some people are focused on their businesses, their work, and taxes, while other people are more concerned about things like lifestyle and weather.

And so on.

This is why it's really important to not 100% copy someone else. They probably can give you good information, but they could have different priorities than you. Instead, you need to do your own research based on the ten factors below and then make your own decision.

The Ten Factors

There are ten major factors you need to consider when picking your ideal country. Some of these factors won't apply to you and you're free to ignore those, but others will be very important to you, meaning you need to consider them very carefully. I will specify when and when it does not apply to you in the factor descriptions. They are listed here in no particular order.

Factor 1: Do you like it after spending at least a week there?

Your first mission is to research online for countries you will like based on these ten factors, then pick the one you are most interested in, and go there for an entire week (though longer is better). Don't stay in a hotel. Stay in an Airbnb or similar and pretend that you live there. Go by real groceries at the grocery store and prepare our own food in your kitchen. Talk to people. Drive around. See stuff. Experience it.

After one week (or more) of experiencing the place, you'll know if you love it, like it, are bored by it, or hate it.

If you are bored by it or hate it, then you'll have to visit the second country on your list, stay *there* for a week, and repeat the process. Usually, you'll fall in love with one of the first two countries because you're doing the analysis I laid out in this chapter, raising the odds that you will like the country or countries you visit.

Factor 2: Does your significant other like it?

If you're 100% single and alone, you can skip this factor.

If you are with someone, you're going to have to determine if they will at least tolerate this place if you decide to move there with them in the future. If you love the country but your wife hates it, that's not going to work.

Once you've made your final decision that this is the country you want (with a second-choice country in case your significant other hates it), he or she needs to visit that country for at least several days so you can confirm everything is alright with them. If it isn't, you'll have to pick a second country and repeat the process until you find a place you both like.

Factor 3: Cost of Living

The country needs to be a place you can easily afford on your current income. If you're extremely poor then you probably don't want to move to Lichtenstein or Monaco. If you're wealthy then super cheap, rougher places like Bolivia or Cambodia probably won't make you happy (though I realize there are always exceptions to these assumptions and I could be wrong).

Also, you need to determine how important the cost of living is to you. Are you moving specifically to save money on lifestyle? Or is that not a priority for you at all? Or are you somewhere in between? There is no right or wrong answer, the point is you need to determine how important this is for *you.*

You can use websites like Numbeo, Expatistan, and Livingcost to do some research on cost of living comparisons between your current collapsing Western country and the new countries you're looking into. Once you spend a week visiting your research countries you'll also see very quickly how cheap or expensive it is to live there.

Factor 4: Climate

This is a tricky one. Most countries in the world have fabulous weather at certain times of the year and absolutely horrible weather at other times. (Both of my homes, Dubai and Paraguay, happen to fall into this category, so this is pretty common.) If you truly hate hot weather or cold weather, then you need to avoid countries like this, but you also need to know if there are several months a year when your target country is either way too hot or too cold for you. And when I say "too cold," it doesn't have to mean cold temperatures; instead, it can mean overall shitty weather, like lots of clouds and rain. This would be places like London or Seattle; they're not *cold* per se, but cloudy and rainy weather is common and persistent.

The first time you visit a new country for research, go when the weather is best. If you love it, then your second visit should be when the weather is at its worst. This way you can see if you can handle it or not.

If you are going to have two or more homes that you're going to cycle through, then this is less important provided the bad weather at both places doesn't happen at the same time. As I've already said, Dubai is extremely hot from June through September and Paraguay is hot from November through February, so this works out perfectly for me; I just always make sure I'm in the country where the weather is nice at the time so I have year-round nice weather, the classic "snowbird" lifestyle.

But if you're planning on being more rooted to one place year-round, you need to ensure the year-round weather is tolerable for you.

Factor 5: Taxes

If you make very little money right now, you can skip this factor for now, though it will become more important as your income grows.

To ensure our Fortress Taxes, meaning paying less than 15% on all taxes you pay in any given year, you need to ensure your new country is tax-friendly. As I already described back in Chapter 8, there are only three types of countries that I consider "tax-friendly":

- Countries with *zero* taxes meaning they don't charge you taxes at all (Bahamas, Monaco, Saudi Arabia, and many others).
- Countries with *microscopic* taxes meaning they have a few very tiny taxes you might or might not have to pay (Montenegro, UAE, Bulgaria, and many others).
- *Territorial tax* countries, meaning there are no taxes on any income you have that comes from outside of the country (Philippines, Belize, Singapore, Paraguay, and many others). This applies directly to your location-independent Alpha 2.0 business, which will generate income from outside of the country, meaning no taxes need to be paid by you.

If a country is in none of those three categories (and virtually no Western countries are), then you can't use that one and need to keep looking. The only exception is if you have multiple homes and don't stay in any one home for more than 182 days per year, since many countries that tax your worldwide income will only do so if you stay there more than six months per year (though there are exceptions to this, like the USA and Australia).

Also, don't forget about VAT or sales taxes. Some oddball countries like New Zealand have massive VAT taxes (like 15% or more) on most items. Living in a country where you pay no income tax but pay massive VAT or sales taxes doesn't make much sense.

Factor 6: Dating Conditions

If you're in a committed, long-term, monogamous relationship, or if you are extremely old, you can skip this factor if you wish.

If you're neither of those things, then likely you'll want a country where there are dating opportunities you would like.

Just for the moment, I'm going to assume you're a man since it's usually men who are more interested in the topics this book covers (if you're a woman, I apologize; please allow me this short and temporary foray into the world of men).

Various men like various kinds of women. Some men love Asian girls, others prefer Latina women, others prefer blonde Eastern European types, and so on. Some men like women with big boobs and/or big asses, while others like a more skinny look. The point is, you already know what you like. So if dating is a priority for you, obviously you need to choose a country where the women have the look that you're attracted to.

There are wild and extreme differences between the appearance of women in different countries, *even if they're in the same region.* For example, I can say "Latinas" but women in Colombia don't look anything like women in Paraguay, women from Mexico don't like either of those, and women in Argentina don't look like any of those three, even though they're all countries with "Latina" women. The same goes for Asian women (Filipino women look absolutely nothing like Japanese women), European women (British women don't look anything like Romanian women), and so forth.

On top of that, you have multicultural countries like the UAE and Singapore where there are tons of different types of women living there.

Also and of course, it's not just about physical appearance, but also about dating *culture.* Dating a Latina woman living in Colombia is a completely and radically different experience than dating an Eastern European woman living in Belarus. These women are going to have very different views and attitudes regarding dating, men, sex, marriage, money, having kids, and so on. You should be aware of these differences.

If you're a man and want more info on dating and relationships for men living abroad, you can to alphamale20.com which is one of my other companies. Lots of resources there that will help you.

Factor 7: Business Conditions

Ideally, you want your new country to be friendly to business owners and possess a strongly growing economy. I say "ideally" because your income is or will be 100% location-independent, you could argue that the local economy of your country isn't relevant since all of your income will be derived from customers/clients outside of your country. This is technically true. I like to live in countries with growing economies instead of stagnating or collapsing economies, but that's just me. Make your own decision on this, based on how important (or not) this factor is to you.

However, regardless of growing, stagnating, or collapsing economies, your country still needs to be friendly to business owners, respect property rights, and follow rule of law, at least as much as possible since no country is perfect on all three of those things. The last thing you want is to move to a new country while reliant on your location-independent Alpha 2.0 business only to have that new country suddenly seize your business or slap huge taxes, fines, or regulations on you or your company.

Again, this doesn't mean your country needs to be perfect in this respect because no country in the world is. Using my two examples of the UAE and Paraguay, these two countries do respect business owners and property rights, however, the UAE sometimes requires hordes of irritating paperwork, and sometimes bribery is part of Paraguayan culture. So *perfection isn't the goal*; just an overall strong sense of a pro-business environment is.

Factor 8: Ease of Travel

If you intend on moving to your new country and just planting yourself there for 12 months a year and not traveling much, then you can skip this factor.

Otherwise, you need to fully understand how easy it is to travel from your country to other major countries, particularly other countries you plan on visiting often.

For example, a lot of Americans and Canadians like flags like Mexico and Panama because they represent quick, direct flights back to the USA or Canada and use the same time zones. Lots of Europeans like Dubai and lots of Australians like Hong Kong and Singapore for the same reasons.

Using tools like Google Maps, Flightconnections.com, and Google Flights, take some time and map out how long flights are to and from your favorite flags. Also note how many stops flights tend to have, where those stopovers are, and how much the flights generally cost. If things look ugly then you may want to reconsider.

For example, one of the biggest reasons I chose Dubai as my primary home was that it is one of the best, if not *the* best travel hubs in the entire world. Living in Dubai, I can fly *nonstop, meaning no stops or layovers, to over 260 cities(!).* Simply incredible. I'm also less than 7 hours away from pretty much all of Europe, the entire Middle East, most of Africa, and almost all of Asia.

Paraguay is another story. Traveling to and from there is somewhat difficult. However, in terms of Paraguay, *I like that.* I like the fact that it's hard to get to, meaning it's "off the radar" from most people and governments of the world, perfect for my escape plan in case something ever goes weird with Dubai or the rest of the planet.

Time zones may also be a factor for you. If you want to be available in the time zones of your former country (and perhaps you don't care), then you need to account for this.

Once again using myself as an example, I like to be at least somewhat accessible to North and South American time zones year-round because it tends to make my life easier both personally and professionally. When I'm in Paraguay this is easy because it's in South America and is in the USA's Eastern Time Zone or close to it depending on Daylight Savings Time and the time of year. When I'm in Dubai, I stay up until 1:30 AM every night and sleep in until 10:00 AM (getting my precious 8.5 hours of sleep every night) which keeps me accessible all day until 5 PM EST for those in North and South America, which works well enough for me. It also gives me an excuse to experience more of Dubai at night which is amazing and looks like something out of a Blade Runner movie.

If you don't care about being accessible to certain time zones, and most people don't, then this isn't a factor. But if it is, make sure you figure that out before you make any solid decisions.

Factor 9: Friendliness to Foreigners

When you're an expat living or spending lots of time in another country, you're a foreigner, so you need to account for how well you'll be treated by the locals on a day-to-day basis.

Not all countries treat foreigners the same way. When it comes to this, they fall into one of five broad categories:

1. Countries who *hate* foreigners. They tend to treat foreigners poorly. Example: France.

2. Countries who *tolerate* foreigners. They are more or less polite to foreigners, but they consider you as beneath them, do things like badmouthing you behind your back as soon as you leave the room, and they will never 100% accept you. Example: Japan.
3. Countries who are *neutral* to foreigners. They don't treat foreigners any better or worse than the natives, at least for the most part. In other words, being a foreigner in that country doesn't help you or hurt you. Example: United States.
4. Countries who *like* foreigners. They treat foreigners with genuine kindness, warmth, and respect, often better than the locals. Example: Paraguay.
5. Countries who *love* foreigners. They are extremely excited whenever they see foreigners and will smile, wave, and shower you with love and joy damn near anywhere you go even, and this is important, when they have absolutely no financial incentive to do so. Example: Fiji.

It should go without saying that you want your country to be in category three, four, or five and you can't have it in category one. Having it in category two (countries who tolerate foreigners) should only be an option for you if you absolutely *love* the country *and* its culture *and* you're reasonably introverted *and* don't require a lot of dating or a large social circle there.

Factor 10: Cultural Acclimation

This one is a little complicated because it involves three sub-factors. Think of each of these as a number between one and ten.

The first sub-factor is a country's *cultural acclimation score*. This is a measurement of how different the culture and lifestyle of your new country are from your original country.

For example, an American moving to Canada will require virtually zero cultural acclimation because the culture of Canada is almost identical to the USA. He'd have no problem adjusting to that lifestyle at all and it would occur almost effortlessly. So for him, Canada would have a cultural acclimation score of 1, or extremely low.

However, if this same American moved to Romania or Ecuador, there would be a lot more cultural acclimation work to do. It would take more time for him to adjust. That being said, Romania and Ecuador are at least somewhat Western cultures, so there likely wouldn't be any massive culture shock either. They would have a cultural acclimation score of about 5 or 6, which would be significant but not an extreme amount.

If that same American moved to Pakistan, he's going to deal with a massive adjustment period because life in Pakistan is almost like living on a different planet than living in the USA. It might take him two or perhaps even three years to adjust to the culture, and even then he'd only be 90-95% adjusted and would probably never be 100%. This would be a cultural acclimation score of 10, extremely high.

Is a high cultural acclimation score bad? Not necessarily. That depends on your personality.

If you have a very *adventurous* and *flexible* personality, moving to (or spending many months a year in) a country with a high cultural acclimation score would not be a negative for you; on the contrary, it would probably be a very exciting and rewarding experience *for you*. But if you're the kind of person who is more picky or stubborn and wants a more predictable lifestyle, moving to a place like that would make you very unhappy.

So you need to rate your *adventurousness* on a scale from one to ten, and then do it again for your *flexibility*.

Be honest about this! If you are not a particularly flexible or adventurous person, there's nothing inherently wrong with that; put down lower scores if that's really who you are. If you lie to yourself about this, you may end up moving to a country that will irritate the hell out of you.

I'll use myself as an example again. My adventurousness score used to be 10 when I was a young man. Now that I'm in my fifties, it's dropped to about an 8, which isn't 10 but is still pretty high. My flexibility score is 9. As I type these words I'm in my very small one-bedroom apartment in Dubai that would drive a lot of Westerners crazy. With my income, I could afford something ten times larger, even in Dubai, but I'm very flexible about these kinds of things so I don't care. I also live in Paraguay 4-5 months a year which many Westerners would consider a third-world country... and it doesn't bother me at all because I'm both adventurous and very flexible.

Many years ago I strongly considered moving to Hong Kong, which for an American has a pretty high cultural acclimation score of 7 or 8. I also seriously considered moving to China at one point, which, for an American, would have a cultural acclimation score of at least 9.5 if not a full 10. Either of those places would be okay to move to *for me* because my adventurousness and flexibility scores are pretty high. If you had an adventurousness score of 3 and a flexibility score of 2, and many Westerners do, then these countries would be nightmares for you if you had to live there year-round.

When you rank these three scores, don't worry about being 100% accurate. We're just guessing here and that's okay. If you're having trouble assessing what your adventurousness and flexibility scores are, then be aware that most Westerners, especially modern-day Americans, tend to have medium flexibility scores but very low adventurousness scores. When talking about a possible new country, some Westerners (and Americans in particular) will say things like:

What if I move there and there's a war?
What if I get killed by terrorists?
What if I do something wrong or say something they don't like and the cops throw me in jail?
What if I get kidnapped or killed by cartels?
What if I get some kind of disease? Do they have good hospitals there?
What's the water quality like there?
Do they respect gun rights?

If you're saying or thinking any of these kinds of things this indicates you have a low adventurousness score, as in 3 or less. As I said, most Americans suffer from extremely low adventurousness, though other Westerners, like Australians, tend to be more adventurous.

Once you have your adventurousness and flexibility scores, now you know what level of cultural acclimation you will be happy with. If these scores are high, you can move to just about any culture you want and you'll probably be fine. If one or both are low, then you should try to stick with countries that have cultures that are not massively different from what you're accustomed to.

One small, possible exception to this are *expat enclaves*. In some countries, expats from a particular country will cluster and form mini-societies where much of their home cultures are retained. For example, there are Americans who live full-time in Mexico in wealthy, American-only, gated communities where everyone speaks English and life is very American-like. There are similar enclaves of Americans in the Tsim Sha Tsui region of Kowloon in Hong Kong. In Paraguay, there are enclaves of Dutch, Germans, and even Koreans.

I don't recommend living in an expat enclave, but that's just my personal opinion. I'm just stating that living in an enclave like this can "short circuit" much of a country's high acclimation sore.

Okay, that covers the ten factors. However, there are a few more rules you need to pay attention to when selecting your ideal country.

The Adjacent Enemy Rule

One requirement for any living flag where you are going to spend six months per year or more is the Adjacent Enemy Rule. This rule states that you can't live in any country that borders another country that is warlike or that hates its neighbor. The reason for this is that you may take all the time and effort to move to this country only to have to deal with invading tanks or flying missiles just a few years later. Obviously we don't want that, so we need to make sure that the country you move to is safe from war from any adjacent asshole neighbors.

"Adjacent" means the country must touch the border of the enemy country. If there is a problematic country somewhere *in the region* but it doesn't border your country, then this is acceptable and the Adjacent Enemy Rule doesn't apply.

For example, the United Arab Emirates where I live. The UAE only borders two countries, Saudi Arabia and Oman, two of the UAE's strongest allies. This makes the UAE quite safe and it passes the Adjacent Enemy Rule with flying colors.

However, some nervous, low-information people unfamiliar with the Middle East might say, *"But what about Iran???"* Iran is indeed a warlike and aggressive country. But in terms of the UAE, it's in the region, but it's not adjacent. Iran is on the other side of the Arabian Gulf, putting a large body of water between us, making an attack from Iran by ground impossible here in Dubai. Moreover, Iran has no desire to attack the UAE; they're more focused on Israel which is nowhere near the UAE, and Saudi Arabia which is a huge country with no major cities anywhere near the UAE.

If, for some very bizarre and microscopically low-odds reason Iran suddenly launched missiles at Dubai (why the hell would they do that?) the UAE has a missile defense shield every bit as good or better than Israel's which has been tested many times and has proven to work amazingly well. On top of that, the UAE's air force is vastly superior to Iran's which wouldn't stand a chance. Iran knows all of this.

(As a side note, it's hilarious to me when people living in the Collapsing West worry about my safety from war living in the UAE. If you live in the USA, Canada, Western Europe, or similar, there are literally *dozens* of Chinese and Russian long-range nuclear ICBMs pointed at your home *right now*. There are *none* pointed at me here in Dubai. And none pointed at me when I'm in Paraguay either. Yet again, I am more safe than Westerners from the very things people living in the Collapsing West are worried about.)

Unfortunately, the Adjacent Enemy Rule crosses off many otherwise fine countries from our potential list of long-term living flags. Armenia is one of my strongest flags and one of my favorite countries, but unfortunately, it borders Azerbaijan, a country that hates Armenia and tends to attack it from time to time, making Armenia fail the Adjacent Enemy Rule and disallowing me to spend more than six months a year there. Estonia, Latvia, Lithuania, Georgia, and several other decent countries border Russia. The problem is that Russia is run by a murderous and aggressive dictator who likes to attack bordering countries whenever hell he wants, often does so, and no one does anything to stop him. Thus, *all* countries bordering Russia fail the Adjacent Enemy Rule no matter how good they are in other respects.

You should also apply the Adjacent Enemy Rule to countries facing civil war and/or similar internal military threats. This would include countries like Venezuela and Israel; no matter what else you may like about these countries (and there is a lot to like about those two), they're just too dangerous for the long-term future.

I could list many more examples of violations of the Adjacent Enemy Rule but you get the point.

To be clear, if a country borders an angry or warlike neighbor, you *can* still use it for other flag purposes, like for your Country B or Country C if you're doing Five Flags, or if you want to get a backup residency there, or if you like to visit there for vacations or dating purposes. You just can't live there for more than six months a year. As I said, I use Armenia for several flag purposes and will continue to do so; I just don't *live* there.

The Chaos Rule

Some countries are extremely chaotic. Their economies, cultures, currencies, and/or infrastructure constantly bounce up and down in huge and unexpected swings like super balls. Their voters are totally insane and elect crazy politicians and vote for ridiculous laws. Their governments are ridiculously disorganized, volatile, and corrupt, more than most other governments. Crime is often really bad, then it's safe, then it's really bad again.

The Chaos Rule states that if you decide to live there, that's okay, but you need to ensure that 100% of your finances and income are *not* based inside that country. This is to protect you against that chaotic country's near-constant internal problems and mood swings.

Examples of chaotic countries include Brazil, Argentina, El Salvador, Puerto Rico, South Africa, Albania, Myanmar, and a few others. If you choose to make any of those your living flag, take the proper precautions. Make sure you have no customers or clients there. Make sure all of your savings, cash, and investments are not there. Avoid using their currencies as much as is feasible. Make sure your living conditions are safe and you live in a safe part of town, and so on. If you don't want to worry about all of these precautions, then don't live in a chaotic country and instead use it as a vacation spot, dating flag, or some other purpose.

Chapter 15

Dealing With Your Fear and Objections To Internationalizing

I've been discussing these topics with thousands of people for over a decade. I have found that the biggest obstacle to saving yourself, making a brighter and safer future for yourself and your loved ones, and making these changes in your life have nothing to do with how to do it. Instead, 80% of the barriers are *inside your head.* At this point in the book, you've probably come up with various reasons, objections, excuses, fears, and concerns that may prevent you from starting your own Alpha 2.0 business or internationalizing.

The good news is that I've heard every objection possible and I can tell you for a fact that 90% of them are based on falsehoods and misinformation. Westerners in general and Americans in particular are notorious for not knowing jack shit about the world outside of the Collapsing West. Many base their opinions on two or three articles or YouTube videos instead of hard data or on-the-ground experience.

Even the remaining 10% of valid objections often have easy workarounds.

Also, *you* may not have any of these objections per se but you might have heard other people in your personal life or on the internet make these objections. And if you haven't heard any of these objections from others yet, you definitely will as you build your Fortress. Instead of worrying that they might be right, this chapter will set you straight.

In this chapter, I will list every major objection I've ever heard and their answers to it. I'm quite sure your fears or objections, if you have any, will be addressed in this chapter, so you can rest easy once you're done reading it. Here they are, listed in no particular order

None of this will help because if the USA/West collapses, the entire planet Earth will go down with it. It doesn't matter where you live, Western Collapse will destroy literally everything everywhere.

Factually incorrect.

Many Westerners, particularly Americans, incorrectly believe that if the USA/Europe/Canada/whatever part of the Western world they love collapses, then the entire planet Earth is completely screwed. Yep, they say, if America goes under, then every one of the other 195 nations of the world instantly collapses as well, so we're all fucked no matter where we are.

The reality is that as shocking as it is for many Americans to hear, some entire nations and economies aren't tied to the USA or the West at all.

I'm typing these words in my second home in Paraguay. I can tell you for a fact that if the United States completely collapsed tomorrow morning, sure, *you'd* be screwed if you lived in the USA, but people in Paraguay *wouldn't even notice it happened.* They'd certainly see it on the news and discuss it, and then they'd go right back to their lives with no noticeable difference. There might be a handful of attorneys or international bankers in Paraguay who might have a temporary disruption in their income, but 99% of people there would be just fine and completely unaffected. This is one of the reasons I use Paraguay as one of my flags; it will be protected when the West collapses.

Let's take my primary home in Dubai. Would Dubai be affected if the USA collapsed tomorrow? Yes, it would; there would certainly be some problems there if that happened. Would Dubai or the UAE completely *collapse* because of it? No. Its economy is strong, taxes and business regulations are low, and everyone in the world wants to move there and none of that would change. There's zero crime, zero wokeism, zero homeless people, and zero social unrest. Its government has very little debt and trillions in assets. Most of its biggest trading partners are not Western and many of them don't do any (or very little) business with the West; places like Iran, Iraq, Russia, India, and Saudi Arabia. Dubai would go through a few years of adjustment and there would be some temporary pain, and then it would be fine. It could actually benefit from such a collapse in the long run.

The West will collapse in your lifetime, but the world outside the West will go on.

None of this internationalizing stuff is going to protect me against AI. AI will take over the entire world!!!

First off, you're assuming that the utopians are 100% accurate about the AI Communist Utopia. They might be right, but they might be wrong and this may never happen. **You don't know.**

Secondly, AI to that degree is going to need a massive amount of first-world infrastructure that simply doesn't exist in many regions outside of the West. Sure, AI could take over a place like New York City, London, or Tokyo in a high-tech, first-world country pretty easily, but how the hell would it do that in a place like the Philippines? It can't. The required infrastructure doesn't exist. Many people in countries like that don't even have things like paved roads or running water, much less ubiquitous high-speed wifi, massive, Tesla-like manufacturing facilities, or armies of Boston Dynamics robots.

Even if you argued that the AI overlords will eventually get there "someday," it would be one of the last places on Earth where this would happen. Remember what I said about being the "last man standing" in the AI chapter? You are *guaranteed* to be among the first people this happens to if you live in or near any Western first-world city, but I could easily be one of the last people to experience it in the world in my home in Paraguay.

Traveling to other countries is too expensive.

If you have no money and no income then of course this is an issue and you need to go make some money first, but I have a feeling you're not in that category.

A lot of people vastly overestimate the cost of traveling internationally. The most expensive part of international travel is the plane ticket since you can get lodging for very cheap just about anywhere with a little planning. However, if you hunt hard enough, you can find a plane ticket that will take you damn near anywhere in the world for less than $800, often as low as $500.

Secondly, if you travel regularly and use the correct credit cards, you'll quickly rack up lots of frequent flyer miles, so much of your travel will be free.

Thirdly, you're likely to save a massive amount of money on taxes; this will often more than pay for some or all of your travel expenses.

This is pussy shit! I'm not going to cut and run like some coward! I'm going to stay and fight for my country! That's what a real man does!

If you really believe this, you need to stop right now, take a deep breath, center yourself, turn on your brain, and go back and reread Chapters 3 and 4, and do so very slowly. Countries in the Collapsing Trifecta, especially the USA, can't be saved at this point no matter who you elect, what movements you start, or how loudly you or people like you scream on social media. It's mathematically impossible.

"Staying and fighting" for a country you *already lost* and that *can't be saved* is foolishly irrational at best and idiotic at worst. I know your emotions are raging about this, but it's just that: *emotions.* Emotions are not objectively and factually accurate to the real world.

If you want to stay on a sinking ship and drown with everyone else just because you loved what the ship used to be 40 years ago, then go right ahead, but you're clearly insane. I'd rather you live and be happy, but that's me.

I've compared these modern-day "stay and fight" right-wingers to the old Japanese soldiers they found on small islands in the South Pacific in the 1960s. These guys thought World War II was still being fought and that they still had a chance of winning, when in fact the war had ended over 20 years ago and they lost.

The country you're trying to "fight for" is already long dead. And it's never coming back. Accept it, and take action to live a better life.

You can only get legal residency in a country if you live there for a few years.

Incorrect. In countries like the UAE, Armenia, Paraguay, Mexico, Panama, and several others, you can get full legal residency without ever having to live there and even without having to go there very often. I gave you the full list back in chapter 13. It's true that in most countries in the world, you have to live there to get legal residency. Great, don't choose those for things like international backup plans.

Americans have to pay taxes even if they move out of the country so there's no point in doing any of this for them if the goal is saving money on taxes.

Incorrect. While the Collapsing USA is the only nation in the world (besides Eritrea which no one cares about) that forces you at gunpoint to pay taxes to its government even if you leave the USA and never go back (shit, and people still think the USA is a "free" country), the first $130,000 you earn per year is 100% tax exempt if you do it correctly. That means if you make less than that, you're going to pay *zero taxes to the USA*. If you make more than that, you can still deduct that amount from your taxable income. Plus, this $130,000 figure increases every year.

In addition to all of that, there are other things you can do to legally save money on taxes beyond that if you're international based on how you structure your corporations, which we'll discuss in Chapter 16.

Americans can save massive amounts of money on their taxes by leaving the Collapsing USA, even if they don't renounce their citizenship. I did.

I would love to do this but I have no idea where to start or what countries I would like.

I showed you how to do that in Chapter 14.

I would love to do this but I have small children.

I addressed that in detail in Chapter 13 under the Family Factors section.

What about my family??? If my country collapses while I'm safe far away and they're still there, then they'll be in trouble! I can't abandon them!!! That's mean!!!

Take them with you. I know people who have brought their parents or siblings along with them. It works out fine.

If they don't want to go, then that's their decision. They're adults and can make their own choices. If you show them that their country is in trouble long term and they ignore that and choose to stay, then that's on them. Saying it's "mean" to leave them doesn't make any sense. What's the alternative? Go down with the ship with them?

You're in a burning house. Your elderly dad is sitting on his chair in the living room.

You say, "Dad, let's go! The house is burning down!"

Your dad replies, "Fuck you! This is my home! I'm not going anywhere! And Trump just got elected again so he'll fix it!"

"But Dad," you scream, "You're going to DIE! The house is burning down!"

"No I won't!" he yells back. He refuses to leave.

So what are you going to do? Are you going to knock him out and physically force him to get on the plane with you to move to another country? No.

Are you telling me you're going to stay in the burning house and die with your dad because you love him? That sounds pretty insane to me.

I would do my absolute best to convince my dad to leave, showing him all the facts and data and how great it would be long-term for him, but if he still refused to leave, then I would leave, because I want to live. And if he later died (figuratively in this case), that would be sad, but I did what I could and he made his own decision. I'm not going to (figuratively) die for my bitchy mom, stubborn dad, asshole brother, brainwashed adult daughter, pussy-whipped best friend, or whoever doesn't want to leave their collapsing Western country. You shouldn't either.

Are your loved ones important? Of course! However, as I already addressed in great detail in Chapter 8, not all loved ones should be placed in the same category; many of your loved ones pull you down instead of building you up, even if you love them and they love you.

Other countries are dangerous! I'll get kidnapped, arrested, killed, robbed, or raped if I go there!!!

I'm going to assume you're an American because, in my experience, only Americans make this nonsensical and inaccurate excuse.

This is factually incorrect. There are at least 23 countries that are safer and have less crime than the Collapsing USA. (I know, because I live in one of them, The United Arab Emirates, where we have essentially a 0% crime rate.) There are an additional 30 or so countries that are safer than the USA depending on the region you live in inside those countries. Remember that you would never choose to move to a high-crime area in any country, right?

Moreover, as I talked about in Chapter 3, crime rates, including violent crime, have been rising in the USA since 2019 and get worse every year as the USA gets closer to collapse. The USA is not the safe place it used to be and will continue to get worse.

It is absolutely hilarious to me when people who live in Chicago (for example) say they would never live in a place like Mexico (for example) because Mexico is "too dangerous," when in fact most of Mexico is statistically safer than most of Chicago!

Only in America…

I don't know. This stuff all seems so complicated. What if I pick a country and move there and find out it's the wrong country for me?

I have *never* seen a person move to a new country after doing the research this book suggests and then end up hating it. Seriously, I've not seen *one person* go through this. The worst I've seen is that a person's girlfriend, boyfriend, or spouse had a problem, but if you're single that doesn't apply to you.

But let's say it does happen to you. You do all the research, move to a new country, and decide you hate it. If that happens, then guess what? You just move again. You won't have a bunch of stuff with you from your first move so it won't be a big deal.

If America (or insert any other Western country here) sucks so much then why does everyone in the world want to move here?

Because they live in third-world shitholes. Do *you* live in a third-world shithole? No? Then that doesn't apply to *you*, does it?

If I was born in Honduras, then you can bet your ass I would do everything in my power to move to the Collapsing USA even if I had to break 100 laws to do it. I'd then live a less-bad life in a safer, more advanced society even if it was collapsing, and the bankrupt quasi-socialist government there would print up a bunch of dollars, create a bunch of inflation and/or raise taxes on those stupid, brainwashed Westerners already living there to give me a bunch of free money, housing, schooling, childcare, healthcare, food and all kinds of other free stuff. Total win for me!

But I wasn't born and raised in a place like Honduras and you weren't either, so *none* of this is relevant to us. You were born and raised in the Collapsing West, with Western resources, cash, education, and culture. *You are the stupid American* (or stupid Canadian or stupid European or stupid whatever) who's getting raped by your government via politics, regulations, inflation, and taxes so that people from Africa, Central America, or other places can live for free in your country on your hard work.

So yeah, if you live in fucking Somalia then you shouldn't do anything this book is recommending; you should run *toward* the Collapsing West as fast as you can so you can get all of your free shit from those stupid, socialist Westerners. But if you already live in the Collapsing West, you need to get the hell out of there.

The Five Flags stuff seems like way too much work.

You're right, it *is* too much work… if you make less than about $180,000 a year. As I've said, full-on Five Flags is only for people with more financial resources and serious motivation. That won't be everyone. If you're a lower or medium-income person, don't bother with Five Flags and instead focus on the other internationalizing levels like setting up an international backup plan, which is doable on any income with a little pre-planning.

You said Colombia (or insert any other non-Western country here) is a good place to live, but you're stupid! I was born and raised in Colombia and I'm still here now! It's a HORRIBLE place because of X, Y, and Z!

You're right. Colombia, and many other non-Western countries, absolutely suck… for people born and raised in Colombia. Once again, were *you* born and raised in Colombia? No? Then guess what? As a Westerner, Colombia is one of the best places in the world to live for a myriad of reasons. The same goes for the Philippines, Cambodia, Paraguay, and many others.

Yeah, these countries aren't exactly a cakewalk for people who were born there, raised there, have little to no education, are saddled with a weak economy and currency, and are stuck there. But for you, the location-independent Westerner with Western income, these are utterly fantastic places (or can be).

What if all of your predictions are wrong? What if the USA/Canada/Europe never collapsed and went on to become prosperous societies? Won't you feel dumb by missing out because you're not there?

Firstly, go back and re-read Chapter 3 very slowly, then provide me with your rational, fact-based arguments, with links and stats to back up what you're saying, as to why you think any country in the Collapsing Trifecta is going to suddenly become prosperous any time soon. I don't think you can do that. I'm sorry, but the West is fucked.

Secondly, if, for some bizarre, magical, Disney fairytale reason the USA/Canada/Europe suddenly booms economically and becomes a paradise, *that would be the ideal scenario for me.* I would stay in Dubai/Paraguay, sell tons of stuff to people living in the West, make shitloads of money, and pay virtually no taxes while enjoying happier cultures. This would be while everyone in the "booming West" would still be paying their 51-70% tax rates and would still be screaming at each other about transgender people or who's going to win the next useless presidential election.

You don't understand that if you escape the Collapsing West and internationalize, *you win no matter what happens.* If the West collapses, you win, because you'll be protected. If the West booms economically, you still win because of your vastly reduced taxes on your Western income, reduced cost of living, and being around happier people.

This is the opposite of those poor bastards still living in the West when the Creeping Darkness and/or the AI Black Hole of Unknown comes knocking at their doors. They *only* win if that *doesn't* happen (and it probably will), but you win *either way.*

Chapter 16

Corporate Structures and Asset Protection

If you are a lower-income person or don't have any real net worth yet, you can skip this chapter. If you do have real location-independent income and/or real assets, then this chapter is for you.

A key part of internationalizing and building your Fortress is arranging your business structures (corporations or the equivalent) to minimize taxes and maximize asset protection of the liquid cash and other assets that reside inside these entities. Protecting your non-corporate assets is also a key factor. That's what we'll cover in this chapter.

There are four ways to save money on taxes and protect your assets through your business while internationalizing. They would be using offshore corporations, tiered corporate structures, international trusts, and stateless assets. I'll cover all four.

Offshore Corporations

In Five Flags parlance, which I covered back in Chapter 12, this would be your Country C. This means that you own a corporation (or the equivalent, like an LLC) in a country where you do *not* live and where you do *not* hold a passport. To be clear, you *can* have legal residency in that country, just not citizenship. Also, you *can* spend time in that country; you just can't live there for more than six months a year.

The benefits of having one or more offshore corporations are tax savings, asset protection, privacy, and financial access.

Tax Savings

Depending on what your Country B is (what passport(s) you hold) and the country where your offshore corporation is located, you possibly stand to save money on taxes that the corporation earns and possibly the amount of taxes you pay when you withdraw funds from that corporation as profit.

Be aware there are two factors at play here.

The first is the *corporate tax the company pays* based on where it's located. In most cases (though not all) this is a tax levied on the corporation's profits before you take any profits out to spend in your personal life. So, if your corporation is in Argentina you're going to pay a 35% corporate tax, but if it's in Lithuania you'll pay a 15% tax, and if it's in Dubai you'll pay a 9% tax if it's over $103,000 USD annually and no taxes if it's under that. Some places have zero percent corporate taxes like the Cayman Islands or British Virgin Islands, though setting up corporations there might take a little more time, effort, or money depending on your situation.

The second factor is the *personal tax you need to pay* after you take the money out of your corporation and have paid the corporate tax. This is based on the country where you live most of the year (your "tax base"). You can't just offshore a company, do nothing else and expect to save a lot of money on taxes because your home country will still demand its cut. You need to add together the corporate tax you would pay plus the personal tax you would pay to get your total tax burden.

For example, let's say your business makes $120,000 USD per year in profit. You are an Australian (with an Australian passport) and you unfortunately live in Authoritarian Australia most of the year. To save money on taxes, you set up an offshore corporation in Lithuania where the corporate tax is 15% instead of Australia's ridiculous 30%. Let's say you're able to save that 15% difference (and I'm no expert on Australian tax law so I don't know if you could or not).

That's great, but we have one big remaining problem: you still live in Authoritarian Australia. Like other Western countries, Authoritarian Australia taxes you personally on your *worldwide* income. So your income from your Lithuanian corporation is still 100% taxable under your personal income tax in Australia.

So you perhaps save some money on corporate taxes, but then as soon as you pull the money out of your offshore corporation to spend in your personal life, you are immediately slapped with a whopping 45% personal income tax even though the income was from offshore. So was offshoring to Lithuania worth the time, effort, and money to do so? Perhaps, but probably not.

Let's take an alternate example. You're German with a German passport and you make around $200,000 USD a year in profit from your company. You leave Germany and move to Dubai, which has a zero percent income tax. Then you set up a corporation in the British Virgin Islands which has an effectively zero percent corporate tax. So your $200,000 in profit gets taxed zero in the British Virgin Islands, then you take it out as profit into your personal life, and Dubai taxes you zero personal income tax. Congratulations, you now pay

ZERO TAXES, 100% legally. (And yes, you could nitpick this and say there are some fees you might have to pay to make all of this work, and you'd have a 5% VAT you'd have to pay in Dubai, but you get my point.)

Asset Protection

This one is obvious. Let's say you are an American living in the Collapsing USA and someone sues you or you go through a really bad divorce. The court and the lawyers can easily go after your house in the USA, your checking accounts in the USA, and all of that other stuff. But if you have $400,000 USD sitting in your Dubai corporation, or have a rental apartment in Cambodia, or gold coins in a vault in Hong Kong owned by a Hong Kong corporation, how are they going to get that stuff? Right. They can't, *even if they know those assets are there.* I mean seriously, is some courtroom in Iowa going to order the Cambodian government to sell that apartment so you can pay some plaintiff? They can't; they have no power there.

Are there some scenarios where a powerful Western body like the US government can seize assets outside of their own country? Sure, it's *possible*, however:

1. The foreign country needs to be a very friendly, allied, cooperating, almost subservient country to the seizing country. For example, the USA could potentially seize funds held in a UK bank account, but it could never do so from an account in Thailand or Paraguay.
2. Even if the foreign country is cooperating, the process is extremely difficult, expensive, paperwork intensive, and time-consuming for both parties and thus is only done in extreme or unusual cases.

So bottom line, your assets are far safer far away from your home or former home country in a foreign corporation than they are if they were held in that country.

Privacy

I'll be honest, this privacy thing is not as strong a feature as it used to be. Most Western countries these days will demand you state most or all of your foreign assets and you're going to (potentially) be in big trouble if you don't. It's also possible for Western countries to look into the bank accounts of other Western countries if needed, per the above. So don't expect to hide all of your assets away from your home or former home government just by offshoring.

That all being said, you do indeed have a higher potential for financial privacy if you offshore than if you don't. The odds of privacy are more in your favor offshore than they are in your country.

Financial Access

This one is huge.

By owning a foreign corporation, you will instantly have access to other key business, financial, or residency options of that country (or other countries) that you wouldn't normally have.

For example, if you want to set up a PayPal or Stripe account but you're a Pakistani living in Pakistan, that might be impossible. But if you set up a foreign LLC in the UK or the USA, now you'll have easy access to all of that stuff through your company, and you might not need to pay any extra taxes to do it because you're not a Westerner.

As another example, if you set up a corporation in a Dubai free zone, they'll immediately hand you full legal residency in the UAE without even having to live there.

The examples of this are too numerous to list. Having an offshore corporation gives you access to all kinds of cool shit in that country (and related countries) that you didn't have before.

Tiered Corporate Structures

If you already make well over $100,000 USD per year, then you may need to look at tiered corporate structures. These are complex to set up and expensive to maintain, but if your income is high enough, it's well worth it because you stand to save massive amounts in taxes.

A tiered corporate structure means you have one corporation in one country that owns another corporation in another country, then often *that* company owns a third company in another country or the first country, and so on. By doing this you can legally avoid large amounts of taxes, far more than the cost of maintaining all of these multiple companies.

There are thousands of possible configurations depending on what country you're from and where you're offshoring to so I can't even begin to list them all, but I'll give you one example to demonstrate how this works. Get ready, because we're about to do some math.

Let's say you're an American who makes $500,000 USD annually in profit from his business and pays the usual 50% or more in taxes to the collapsing government of the USA, which is at least $250,000 a year. This American could instead set up a new C corporation in the USA, then a second corporation in an offshore country that doesn't charge any corporate taxes. The new American corporation could own the foreign corporation. Then he could set up a third corporation (or LLC) back in America again, owned by the foreign corporation (which itself is owned by the American C corporation). Three companies, all owning each other, with the American C corporation at the top.

Then he moves out of the Collapsing USA to a place like Dubai that has no personal income tax.

Once all of this is set up, he takes his first $130,000 as income that is taxed at zero percent because of the USA's Foreign Earned Income Exclusion (FEIE) since he doesn't live in the Collapsing USA anymore. This amount rises every year, so with every year that goes by, he saves even more taxes. The remaining $370,000 in profit he has he either uses towards business expenses (that are taxed at zero percent) or puts into investments that are owned by the American C corporation, again, paying zero taxes because he's not withdrawing any funds from the corporation as personal income (the C corporation owns the investments).

Let's say after all of this, there is still a remaining $185,000 he wants to use as additional personal income for the year. He withdraws that from his American C corporation and gets a 50% deduction in the corporate tax because of a US law that states any C corporation that owns 100% of a foreign corporation only pays half the usual corporate tax rate. As of the time of this writing, America's corporate tax is a flat 21%, so he only pays 10.5% on the $185,000 he withdraws, which is just under $20,000.

To pause for a minute, so far, he's made $315,000 as personal, taxable income and has only paid $20,000 in taxes so far, which is only 6%. He doesn't pay any taxes to Dubai because they don't have a personal income tax.

But we're not quite done. He may have to pay an American personal income tax on the $185,000 he made beyond the FEIE amount of $130,000, but he can do all kinds of things to reduce that via various deductions and will pay perhaps 15-20% on that or less. This means he'll perhaps pay around $28,000 in personal income taxes to the USA. Add that to the $20,000 he's already paid in corporate taxes and that's a total tax bill of $48,000.

So instead of paying over $250,000 in taxes on $500,000 of real profit, he's only paid $48,000, which is a 10.4% tax rate instead of a 50%+ tax rate. Incredible! Even if he has to pay $15,000 a year on fees, accountants, and/or attorneys to maintain all of those companies, it's still well worth it in terms of ROI.

By the way, all of this is 100% legal. There's no money laundering or any of that stuff going on, and we're following all the laws of all the countries involved to the letter.

These examples can get even more complex and crazy for even more tax savings than this. What I just explained above is a relatively simple example.

(Note: I'm not an accountant or tax attorney, so it's possible I may have left out a little tax or two in the above example. Doesn't matter. Doing this will save you tons of money in taxes even if the numbers in my basic example aren't 100% accurate.)

International Trusts

Perhaps the most bulletproof way of protecting your assets is by using international trusts. Under this model, your assets go under a trust which is located in an offshore country. The international trust "owns" the assets instead of you directly owning them. Your name isn't attached to the assets of the trust. Both privacy and asset protection are massive; it's almost impossible for any entity to pierce an international trust. (Note I said *almost* impossible, not impossible. There are no 100% guarantees in life.)

The downside is that international trusts are somewhat expensive to set up. The least expensive good ones that I know of going to cost you at least $35,000 USD and will take several months to set up, in addition to some international travel. However, if you already have millions of dollars in assets you want to protect, $35K (or so) isn't very much and the ROI is probably worth it.

International trusts are a big and complex topic and the details go far outside the scope of this book, so I can't go into detail on them here. Just be aware that this is an option to protect your assets.

Stateless Assets

If you're like most investors, most assets in your portfolio are tied to a specific country. For example, if you own stocks or ETFs in the S&P 500, these are all 100% tied to the United States. If you own a house in Paris, it's tied to France. If you have a bank account full of Euros in the city of Tallinn, that's tied to Estonia directly and the European Union indirectly.

There is nothing wrong with assets tied to a specific country as long as you're careful and you know what you're doing. For example, other than a few bank accounts, I don't have any assets whatsoever in the USA and haven't for many years; no American stocks, bonds, ETFs, or real estate. I don't want assets in a rapidly declining country. On the other hand, I do have assets in Paraguay and I plan on having more in the next few years because that's a rising country. This structure has served me well; since 2017 I've had numerous years where my investments made over 100% in just one year.

All that being said, there is a different type of asset that is not tied to any one country. These are called stateless assets. For example, bitcoin is a stateless asset. It's not tied to any one country or group of countries. No country or group of countries can destroy it, inflate it, or completely ban it (China has tried three times and failed). Moreover, it can be easily transported all over the planet without any country's permission. Bitcoin isn't a perfect asset of course and there are downsides to it since there is no such thing as a perfect asset. Regardless, it is indeed stateless in that, provided you hold bitcoin in a non-custodial wallet and not in an exchange, it is protected from any government or group of governments doing anything stupid like destroying it, banning it, confiscating it, or dramatically harming its value.

"Stateless" is not usually a binary, yes or no thing. Sometimes assets can be partially stateless.

For example, if you own a bunch of gold coins hidden in a safe somewhere in Montenegro, that's a stateless asset because the government of Montenegro has nothing to do with your gold and probably doesn't even know it's there. However, you could argue that it's "a little" related to Montenegro in that if you aren't physically in the country you'd have to fly there to go get your gold. If the government of Montenegro barred you from entering the country for whatever reason, which is unlikely but technically possible, that might be an issue.

That being said, precious metals not stored in a bank (because banks are often tightly controlled by governments) are considered a stateless asset because they mostly are.

Stateless assets, while again not perfect, do offer something that normal assets don't: no government or group of governments have any control over them, and in most cases don't even know you have them. This is a huge plus for you. Privacy, asset protection, long-term protection against governments, and so on.

Here is a list of "full" or "mostly" stateless assets:

- Cryptocurrency (as long as it's not in an exchange)
- Precious metals you own that aren't stored in a traditional bank (like gold, silver, or platinum)

- Commodities you own that aren't stored in a traditional bank (like diamonds or rare earth minerals)
- Many digital assets (like NFTs, domain names, and so on)
- Luxury items you own (like art, antiques, or expensive rare cars)
- Certain DeFi instruments (like DAO or yield farming)
- Certain private contracts (like private loans or phantom equity)

You can have all stateless assets in your portfolio or a mix of stateless plus standard, country-dependent assets, that's completely up to you. I'm just saying that the more stateless assets in your portfolio, the more protected your assets will be from the chaos most stupid governments will create over the next 30 years.

Chapter 17

Time Is Running Out

This is our final chapter together, so I will make it one of the most important chapters in this book, if not *the* most important one.

The key issue to saving yourself from the Creeping Darkness and the AI Black Hole of Unknown and living a more free and low-taxed lifestyle is one of *deadlines*.

If this was 1993 and you wanted to internationalize to protect yourself and live a better life, you'd have all the time in the world. You could spend months, even *years* researching, pondering, planning, thinking about stuff, traveling, and doing whatever. If you didn't set up an international backup plan or move to another country for another ten years, getting around to it by 2003, you'd be perfectly fine. Time was on your side back then. The collapse hadn't yet begun, Western economies were strong, Westerners hadn't yet gone insane, there was no AI threat, and foreigners getting residencies, passports and things of that nature were relatively easy.

None of that is the case today.

It's now deep into the 21st Century, the cultural and economic collapse of the West has begun in earnest, AI gets stronger every day, and governments all over the planet are cracking down on residencies, passports, banking, and other international aspects that they used to allow in the past.

This means **you don't have any more fucking time left**. You need to initiate these things **right now**. To be perfectly honest with you, and I'm not saying this to be hyperbolic because I 100% believe this based on the data, if you have no location-independent income and you haven't internationalized at all yet, **you are already behind schedule and you should be very concerned**.

I've said publicly that if I lived in the Collapsing USA, Cuckoo Canada, or Suicidal Europe right now *and* I had no location-independent income at all *and* I hadn't internationalized at all, I would wake up every morning screaming in terror. I would be scrambling like a crack-addict maniac running around setting up my location-independent business and/or setting up my international backup plan and/or moving out of my country as fast as humanly possible, putting everything else on my life on hold until I got those things done.

And yet, you see the vast majority of Westerners just carrying on with their lives like everything is fine, going to their day jobs, bitching on social media, voting in their useless elections, with no plans to make any real changes in their lives.

Imagine a big countdown clock on the wall. It shows seconds, minutes, hours, days, months and years. Every second, the numbers flip as it counts down to zero. When it finally reaches zero in a few years, which it inevitably will, if you haven't yet built your Fortress, you're fucked. It will be too late to do things like set up a location-independent business or internationalize your life. You waited too long, and you (and your family if you have one) are going to pay the ultimate price like almost everyone else in the Collapsing West.

But it gets even worse. Imagine there are not one, but *four* of these doomsday clocks, all with different lengths in years, all counting down to zero every second of every day. Some of them have reasonably clear time frames so you can see how much time you have left. However, with others, the year indicator is blank, so you don't know how many years you have.

If *any one* of these doomsday clocks hit zero before you have built your Fortress, you're screwed.

Here are the four doomsday clocks.

Doomsday Clock #1 - Internationalizing Gets Harder Every Year And Will Soon Only Be Available To The Super Wealthy

Back in 2008 or even before that, getting foreign residencies, second passports, moving abroad, banking abroad, and so on was really easy. Most countries' laws were quite relaxed about all this. You had tons of easy and cheap options to choose from. Honestly, I envy guys who internationalized back in 1997, 2006 or 2012 when this stuff was so much easier, simpler, and less expensive.

The reality is that for every year that goes by:

- More countries make their residences and passports harder to get.
- More governments increase their paperwork requirements for these kinds of things.
- More governments increase their prices on things like residencies and passports.
- Banks all over the planet get more strict about doing business with expats and foreigners, always using their two favorite excuses, "money laundering" and "terrorism."

- More countries get angry at each other than before, causing more difficulty with internationalizing.

This gets worse every year, without fail.

There were many easy ways to get foreign banking access, residencies, and passports just five years ago that are no longer available. Five years from now many of the options you have now *will be gone.*

I could give you dozens of examples of this from just the past ten years, but here are a few from off the top of my head.

Back in 2018, Paraguay would give you easy residency without having to move there, then once you had it, if you just waited three years, they'd give you a passport, without having to move the country! It was an awesome deal, so I took advantage of it, went down there, and applied for my residency. I could get my *residency* and then have my Paraguayan *passport* by 2021, all without having to move there! I was excited.

As I was waiting for my residency to be approved, their supreme court ruled that instead of just handing out passports like candy, foreigners would now have to live in Paraguay for nine months a year for three years in a row if they wanted a passport.

Shit!

I got the residency, but couldn't get the passport. If I had gotten Paraguayan residency just a few years before that, I'd have a Paraguayan passport right now, but because this stuff gets harder every year, I don't.

Before around 2021, you could go to the country of Georgia, walk into just about any bank there, show them your Western passport, and boom, they'd give you a bank account. You wouldn't need residency or anything else. It was one of the few countries on Earth where you could get a bank account without also having to get legal residency there. But then the libertarians left office in the Georgian government and the socialists returned. Suddenly, you had to hire a local attorney in Georgia and spend several weeks screwing around with legal fees and banks just to open a personal checking account.

The country of Panama was one of the best and easiest residencies to get in the world. Then a few years ago they purposely made the process of getting residency extremely difficult. They quadrupled the amount of paperwork required. They stopped accepting paperwork from their own embassies. They kept changing their residency procedures every year. In the middle of all of this, they completely mishandled the pandemic far worse than the rest of the civilized world.

I still like Panama but it went from being the around third-best flag in the world to being number 20 or so within a period of just two years.

I could go on and on with more examples of things that used to be easy but are now difficult or impossible, but I think you get my point. Every year that goes by makes internationalizing more challenging.

Today, you can internationalize pretty easily as long as you select the right flags. However, I predict that in about ten years the only people who will be able to internationalize in the ways I'm describing in this book will only be the very wealthy, i.e. those worth at least $10 million or more.

Doomsday Clock #2 – Earning Money, As You Currently Understand It, Will Soon Be Impossible Under The AI Communist Utopia

I already discussed this in detail back in Chapter 6. If/when the AI Communist Utopia takes place, you won't be able to "earn" any more money as you currently understand the concept. Any advantages you currently have in the marketplace you use today to make money will no longer be needed by society because AI will do it all better and/or cheaper than you.

Based on estimates I've seen from people who know a lot more about these things than I do (and as always, they could be wrong), **you have approximately ten years to make the money you want to make**. After that, you won't be able to make any more. You'll just be another peon, clonelike drone like the other eight billion people on Earth who have no assets.

You may argue that the AI Communist Utopia may never happen. That's correct, it might happen, but it might not. However, here is an AI scenario that absolutely will happen…

Doomsday Clock #3 – The Ten Years of Brutality Will Begin In Just A Few Years

This is the shortest doomsday clock of them all. To summarize what I already said about this back in Chapter 6, in just a few years, far before the AI Communist Utopia ever happens, scores of millions, if not hundreds of millions of people are going to be put out of work due to AI. Collapsing Western governments, already in too much debt and already on the brink of economic failure, will not have the ability to help these people without imploding.

If you're one of these people when this doomsday clock reaches zero, you're screwed.

If you're not one of these people but your job or business relies on these people, again, you're screwed.

The Ten Years of Brutality could start within just 3-5 years or less.

Are you getting the picture yet about how you don't have any more time to delay getting your Fortress built?

And we haven't even addressed the biggest doomsday clock of them all…

Doomsday Clock #4 – The Final, Economic and Cultural Collapse of Western Civilization

At some point in your lifetime, very roughly between five and 30 years from now, the Collapsing USA, Cuckoo Canada, and Suicidal Europe will experience one or more of the five collapse scenarios I described in Chapter 4. Other major countries may also collapse, including Israel, South Africa, Japan, Russia, and so forth. Other countries like Australia and New Zealand may not fully collapse but will instead experience massive economic and cultural catastrophes that will make you very unhappy if you still live in those countries when these things occur.

You'd better hope to hell that when this doomsday clock reaches zero, you are either already moved out of these countries or at a bare minimum you've got a fully developed international backup plan *plus* make good money via your location-independent Alpha 2.0 business.

The collapse of the Western world will negatively affect at least a billion people, perhaps more. You don't want to be one of them.

I hope you realize by now that you simply don't have any more time left to screw around, make excuses, procrastinate, engage in perfectionism, self-delusion, or analysis paralysis, or hope that your favorite politician will solve all of these problems for you (especially that one whose name starts with the letter "T").

You need to get to work on building your Fortress, right now.

I'll leave you with the same bit of rational positivity that I used at the beginning of this book. Step one to all of this, which is building your own location-independent Alpha 2.0 business, isn't hard. Our students who had no business experience when they started have garnered multiple four and five-figure location-independent clients within just 2-6 months of starting from zero. Go to store.calebjones.com/90DBB to get more information on our 90 Day Business Builder program.

The second step is either moving out of your collapsing Western country or at least setting up an international backup plan. That isn't hard either. I've seen men and women in my audience set up their backup plans or move to a much better country that they love within just six months of starting from scratch. Go to calebjones.com for resources to help you with these important transitions.

You don't have much time left, but you do still have time *if* you take action *right now*.

My mission in life is to help people like you. As Tom Cruise once said, help me help you. Stop blowing this off and making excuses. Get to work. Save yourself. Save your family if you have one (or your future family if you want one later). Join us truly free and sovereign individuals.

It's a great life.

I hope to see you there soon.

SCAN THIS QR CODE TO CHECK OUT THE
90 DAY BUSINESS BUILDER PROGRAM SO YOU
CAN BE MAKING REAL MONEY IN YOUR OWN
BUSINESS, LOCATION-INDEPENDENT, WITHIN
90 DAYS OR LESS.